THE
BODMIN & WADF
RAILWAY

by

C. F. D. Whetmath

Published by
FORGE BOOKS
55 Brookside, Wokingham, Berks., RG11 2ST
Fourth edition 1994

Bodmin in 1886 on the occasion of an inspection by the directors of the London & South Western Railway. The locomotive Bodmin is at the head of a train which includes all the passenger vehicles..

Introduction
Cuckoo Valley

The Bodmin & Wadebridge Railway was a pioneer railway. Although not the first to be constructed in the Duchy of Cornwall, it was the first to use steam power. Its history can be divided into two quite distinct periods: before 1888, throughout which time there were few changes from the early primitive days, and after 1895 when it settled down to being a normal branch line of the London & South Western Railway.

Main line railways came to Cornwall in 1859 when the Cornwall Railway was completed from Plymouth, across the Royal Albert Bridge at Saltash, to Truro, but although it passed within four miles of Bodmin it had no impact on the Bodmin & Wadebridge line. Indeed, north Cornwall continued to rely on the stage coach for contact with the outside world until the North Cornwall Railway reached Wadebridge in 1895.

A thinly-veiled account of the coming of the Bodmin & Wadebridge Railway and its effect on the Camel Valley is contained in Sir Arthur Quiller-Couch's short story "The Cuckoo Valley Railway". Written in the closing years of the last century this evokes the scene of 130 years ago: "The century was still young and ardent when ruin fell on Cuckoo Valley. Its head rested on the slope of a high and sombre moorland, scattered with granite and china-clay; and by the small town of Ponteglos, where it widened out into arable and grey pasture-land, the Cuckoo River grew deep enough to float vessels of small tonnage from the coast at spring tides. I have seen there the boom of a trading schooner brush the grasses on the river-bank as she came before a westerly wind, and the haymakers stop and almost crick their necks staring up at her topsails. But between the moors and Ponteglos the valley wound for fourteen miles or so between secular woods, so steeply converging that for the most part no more room was left at the bottom of the V than the river itself filled. The fisherman beside it trampled on pimpernels, sundew, watermint, and asphodels, or pushed between clumps of *Osmunda regalis* that over-topped him by more than a foot. If he took to wading, there was much ado to stand against the current. Only here and there it spread into a still black pool, greased with eddies; and beside such a pool, it was odds that he found a diminutive meadow, green and flat as a billiard table, and edged with clumps of fern. To think of Cuckoo Valley is to call up the smell of that fern as it wrapped at the bottom of the creel of the day's catch of salmon-peal and trout.

"The town of Tregarrick (which possessed a jail, a workhouse, and a lunatic asylum, and called itself the centre of the Duchy) stood three miles back from the lip of this happy valley, whither on summer evenings its burghers rambled to eat cream and junket at the Dairy Farm by the river-bank, and afterwards to sit and watch the fish rise, while the youngsters and maidens played at hide-and-seek in the woods. But there came a day when the names of Watt and Stephenson waxed great in the land, and these slow people caught the railway frenzy. They took it, however, in their own fashion. They never dreamed of connecting themselves with other towns and a larger world, but of aggrandizement by means of a railway that should run from Tregarrick to nowhere in particular, and bring the intervening wealth to their doors. They planned a railway that should join Tregarrick with Cuckoo Valley, and there divide into two branches, the one bringing ore and clay from the moors, the other fetching up sand and coals from the sea. Surveyors and engineers descended upon the woods; then a cloud of navvies. The days were filled with the crash of falling timber and the rush of emptied trucks. The stream was polluted, the fish died, the fairies were evicted from their rings beneath the oak, the morals of the junketing houses underwent change. The vale knew itself no longer; its smoke went up day by day, week by week, with the noise of pickaxes and oaths."

The reader may have recognized Ponteglos and Tregarrick as Wadebridge and Bodmin respectively. "Q" then goes on to describe how, after a day's fishing in the Cuckoo River, he decided to return to Tregarrick by train from the Dunford (i.e. Wenford) terminus . . ."Presently we turned down a lane scored with dry ruts, passed an oak plantation, and came on a clearing where the train stood ready. The line did not finish: it ended in a heap of sand. There were eight trucks, seven of them laden with granite, and an engine, with a prodigiously long funnel . . . 'Now,' said one of the twins, while the other raked up the furnace, 'you can ride in the empty truck with the lovers, or on the engine along with us – which you like'.

"I chose the engine. We climbed on board, gave a loud whistle and jolted off. Far down, on our right, the river shone between the trees, and these trees, encroaching on the track, almost joined their branches above us. Ahead the moss that grew upon the sleepers gave the line the appearance of a green glade, and the grasses, starred with golden-rod and mallow grew tall to the very edge of the rails. It seemed that in a few more years Nature would cover this scar of 1834 and score the return match against man."

This certainly became true – the line winding among the trees soon became an integral part of the valley. For many years railway enthusiasts visited it to see the Beattie well-tanks, and it is hard to realise that it is over thirty years since they departed. Although there were never regular passenger trains to Wenford, it was possible to write to Waterloo and obtain a permit to travel in the brakevan of the daily goods train; if one was lucky in practice this meant a ride on the engine when out of sight of "authority". It was necessary to see the Station Master at Wadebridge, who made sure that the fare had been paid; this was charged at the same rate as if it was a normal journey so in 1962 the fare for a whole day out to Wenford was six shillings (thirty pence)!

Unfortunately the last trains to Wenford ran in 1983, so the line just failed to celebrate 150 years of operation. However, ten years on there are moves afoot to reopen the Wenford line for clay traffic, and two of the well-tanks survive, so perhaps one day the sound of a well-tank on a train of clay wagons will once again echo round the valley.

Chapter One
Inception

The Bodmin & Wadebridge Railway owed its existence to the foresight of the principal local landowner, Sir William Molesworth of Pencarrow the eighth Baronet and a progressive man who was to become Colonial Secretary in Lord Palmerston's Liberal Government of 1855. In 1831 he engaged at his own expense a civil engineer from Plymouth named Roger Hopkins to prepare a survey for a railway from Wadebridge to Wenford Bridge with branches to Bodmin and Ruthern Bridge. The object of the railway was to convey limey sea sand from Wadebridge up the valley of the River Camel where it was much in demand as a manure. The Bude Canal and Tamar Manure Navigations elsewhere in Cornwall had been conceived with this traffic in mind. Although the Camel Valley is apart from the great mining areas of East & West Cornwall there were a number of mines active at the time from which downward traffic was also expected. In addition to preparing the plans, Hopkins was required to report on the feasability of the scheme. He had had quite considerable experience of railway construction having been engineer to the Monmouthshire and Severn & Wye Tramways over twenty years earlier, and of the Plymouth and Dartmoor Railway since 1826. He presented his report to the provisional committee led by Sir William Molesworth on 6th January 1832. It was highly enthusiastic and was well received. He estimated that £21,882 9s 4d would be required for the construction of a single track railway, of standard gauge, an additional £1,200 being required for an engine and rolling stock and £2,800 for buildings. He concluded his report by saying "I flatter myself I have now succeeded in redeeming my pledge of proving that this railway will confer immense advantages on the inhabitants of this district in general and be a prosperous speculation to the shareholders. It being evident that the farmer, being able to till his land at less cost, and grow larger and better crops, the landlord and tithe-holders must receive a proportionate benefit; poor and way rates will be decreased; and consumers of shop goods, coals, timber, iron, etc., will pay a diminished price for the articles they purchase. The more perfect the communications of a country, the more prosperous it will certainly become, as facility of intercourse is one of the greatest elements of civilised strength. In the general march of affairs, good roads, railways, canals, etc., mark the progress of a country towards wealth and prosperity and wherever they have been executed in the district not already abounding in wealth, they have invariably directed the flow of riches towards it."

The choice of the standard gauge of 4ft 8½ in was unusual in this area; the previous horse railways in the clay district to the south were of 4ft gauge, whilst that of the Plymouth & Dartmoor was 4ft 6in. It is not unlikely that William James, the railway and canal surveyor, may have influenced Sir William Molesworth in this connection as for many years he lived at Bodmin. He had several years previously prepared plans for a railway from Padstow to Fowey, via Wadebridge and Bodmin, and these may have influenced Sir William's desire for a railway. The railway was not the only form of communication that had been proposed for the district, for in

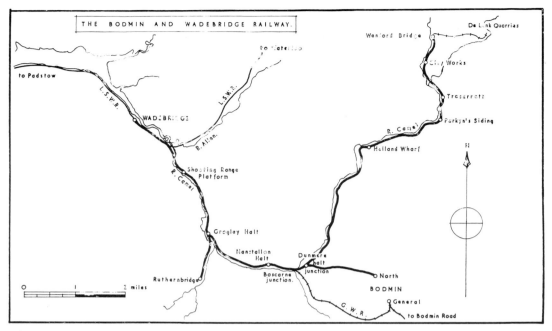

The Bodmin and Wadebridge Railway.

1796 James Murray, under the direction of John Rennie, surveyed the Polbrock Canal, which was to run from Guinea Port, Wadebridge, to Dunmere; although an Act of Parliament was obtained in 1797 nothing further was done at the time.

Upon receipt of Roger Hopkins' Report the provisional committee immediately prepared a bill for presentation to Parliament for "making and maintaining a railway from Wadebridge in the parish of St Breock to Wenford Bridge in the parish of St Breward, with a collateral branch to the Borough of Bodmin, together with certain other branches, all in the County of Cornwall." The Act of Incorporation of the Bodmin & Wadebridge Railway Company (2 & 3 William IV Cap 47) received the Royal Assent on 23rd May 1832. The authorised capital was £22,500, comprising 900 shares of £25 each, with powers to raise loans of up to £8,000. At the first Shareholders' meeting, held at Oliver's Hotel, Bodmin, on the 4th July 1832 it was decided not to exercise these latter until all the shares had been taken up. At the first directors' meeting, on 9th July 1832, Sir William Molesworth was elected Chairman, with John Wallis as Deputy Chairman. The other directors were Dr Harry, Rev T. Grylls, Rev J. Wallis, E. M. Wright, Capt Hext, R. N., Rev J. P. Gilbert, Rev F. J. Hext, F. B. Gambly, John Hooper and Thomas Clarke. The Treasurer was Mr John Pethybridge, Manager of the East Cornwall Bank, Bodmin, and the Clerk was Mr Preston Wallis, a Bodmin solicitor.

On 1st February 1833 the directors resolved to invite tenders for rails and materials, the tenders to be delivered to the Post Office in Bodmin by the 20th of that month. At the meeting it was reported that nine tenders had been received, the majority from South Wales, and also letters from Messrs. Hampton & Co. and the Birmingham Coal & Iron Co. Mr Hopkins suggested that he visited the latter and also Kenrick & Co. of the Varteg Hill Iron Works to discuss terms. This was agreed by the directors, who allotted up to £10 to cover his expenses. Four weeks later, on 18th April, the directors met to hear Mr Hopkins report on the result of his trip to

Bristol. He recommended that the tender of the Yniscedwyn Iron Works be accepted. This, and a tender from Mr Oliver to supply barrows at 50s each were accepted. Three days later the scheme took a major step forward when it was resolved "to proceed forthwith to cut the first turf in a field belonging to Mrs Hickwood and others near Drinnick Bridge".

As on other early Cornish lines, the sleepers were formed of local granite blocks, 20in x 20in x 12in thick, and costing 8d each, except at railjoints, where a single granite sleeper 6ft wide was employed. The iron rails were 15-18 feet long, weighing 42 lbs per yard, and costing £8 and £10 per ton. The chairs in which they rested on the sleepers weighed 10½lbs; at railjoints a larger chair held the ends of each rail, which were retained by iron keys.

It had originally been intended to work the line with horses, but it was later decided to employ a steam engine. In May 1833 a Mr Gurney offered two engines and tenders weighing 5 tons each, and costing £900 each, for delivery at Wadebridge, and to be kept in good order for six months after traffic commenced. Later in the year one of the directors, Dr Harry, was invited to ascertain what would be the most suitable type. After a visit to South Wales he recommended a design of the Neath Abbey Iron Works; following his recommendation, which was accepted by the other directors on 27th September, the engine, subsequently named the *Camel,* was duly ordered. It was assembled at Wadebridge under the supervision of an engineer from the makers.

Progress was slower than had been expected, and it was not until 4th July 1834 that the *Camel* made its first run to Bodmin. Several trips were made during July and August; the first train to Ruthern Bridge, with two wagons, ran on 6th August. The remainder of the 'main-line', from Dunmeer to Wenford Bridge was not publicly opened until Tuesday 30th September, and the official celebrations were reserved for that date. On the inaugural train 300 tickets were issued, for the shareholders and invited guests. The clerk of the railway was instructed to have 20 special constables sworn in, and to place one in each carriage. Each of the special constables was paid 2s, and £10 was allotted to the contractors and workmen for their own celebrations.

The "West Briton & Cornwall Advertiser" of 3rd October 1834 recorded the scene at the opening: "As soon as the different parties were arranged, the procession set out in the following order: a waggon in which were the bricklayers employed in the work, with their tools, preceded the locomotive engine and tender in which sat Messrs Hopkins the engineers, Thomas Woolcombe Esq, and several other gentlemen. To the engine seventeen wagons and an omnibus were attached. These vehicles were tastefully fitted up and decorated with flags, green branches, etc. On one waggon was displayed a flag on which was neatly painted a representation of the engine and waggons attached, with the words 'Science, Prudence and Perseverance' as a motto. The persons who had obtained tickets, and amongst whom were many ladies, took their place in the carriages, the middle one being occupied by the band (Royal Cornwall Militia in full uniform). The arrangements were completed about twelve o'clock when the very beautiful and powerful engine was put in motion and proceeded drawing the long train of carriages amidst the cheers of the multitude occupying every spot that afforded a view of the road, the band playing the National Anthem. By this time the weather had cleared up and the scene defies description, a more grand and imposing sight was

Artist's impression of the inaugural train on 30th September 1834 crossing the Pendavey Bridge.

never, perhaps, witnessed in this county. The train moved forward at the rate of six miles an hour, occasionally increasing its speed to ten miles in the same time until arriving at Dunmeer, 5½ miles from Wadebridge, where a fresh supply of water was taken in, when the procession again moved forward; at Tresarrett another supply was obtained; and at Wenford Bridge which is the termination of the line being twelve miles from Wadebridge, a halt of upwards of half an hour took place in order to arrange for returning to Dunmeer, which being effected in the best style, the engine, after stopping to take in water, etc., as before, ascending the branch to Bodmin, drawing the tender, omnibus and waggons and preceded by the workmen employed on the railway walking two by two, and reached the town at five o'clock amidst the cheers of the multitude assembled to witness the arrival . . . We are most happy to report that not the slightest accident occurred to damp the satisfaction expressed by all who were present."

Although the line to Wenford Bridge was regarded as the main line it never saw passenger trains, except occasional excursions. In the early years, however, passengers were conveyed unofficially in the "tool wagon", an open sided four-wheeled vehicle that was always coupled between the engine and the train, and which had two sets of buffers, one to match the standard buffers fitted to the later engines, and a lower set for use with the old rolling stock. It was also possible to arrange for a passenger coach to be attached to the goods train; picnic parties often asked for an 'open car'. The passenger fares from Bodmin to Wadebridge were 8d "outside" and 1s "inside", single. The company pioneered the issuing of cheap excursion tickets, passengers returning on the same day being charged the single fare for the return journey. The maximum permitted speeds were 6 mph on the "ascending" journey (i.e. from Wadebridge) and 8 mph "descending". Even after it had been decided to employ steam engines it was thought they would be incapable of hauling traffic on the steeply graded Bodmin branch, but a test showed that *Camel* could easily haul three loaded wagons. The later *Elephant* engine could haul four wagons.

The Headquarters were at Wadebridge, the Chief Superintendent and Wharfinger there, Octavius Dunston, being responsible for the day to day running of the line. He received a salary of £100 per annum, later increased after prolonged negotiations to £104. The "Exeter & Plymouth Gazette" reported that the line had opened under favourable conditions, and that plans were being made for extensions to Delabole, Launceston and Calstock on the River Tamar; there were further schemes which would have connected with the Exeter & Crediton Railway.

Chapter Two
Early Days

The Company's Day Books provide a fascinating insight into the day to day running of the railway in the early years, and include details of the traffic handled, and of any unusual events, or mishaps. The first few weeks of regular traffic passed without undue incident, and the *Camel* worked satisfactorily until 15th October 1834, when "in returning, the axle of Feeder broke". Although repaired at Wadebridge it broke again the following day. The engine was not often used on Mondays, which were spent in cleaning. On 15th January 1835 "one pair of wheels of the engine injured by repeatedly getting between the rails – obliged to stop". The 16th and 17th were spent in repairing and changing wheels; on attempting to raise steam on Monday 18th "the pipes leaked so much were unable to do so; took out the first and caulked the pipes, etc." After the very tall chimney had been broken off (presumably by overhanging trees) on the 22nd, and repaired, the pipes continued to leak and *Camel* was stopped for repairs on the 14th February, and again the 16th when the engine was "leaking so much and the plate being cracked it became absolutely necessary to leave part of the train at the Junction and return. Gave up attempting to work the engine and proceeded to take it to pieces by Order of the Directors". *Camel* was under repair for two months as no spare parts were held, and they had to be made and sent by sea from Hayle and Bristol. The traffic was handled by horses, hired by the company at about £2 5s to £2 10s a week and by the traders themselves. The passenger coach, known as the "omnibus," was also horse-drawn.

After a new set of tubes had been fitted, and various other repairs effected, *Camel* was first tested on 15th April, to Guinea Port and back. The following day it went to the "watering place near Polbrock and Ruthern Wharf". Easter Monday, the 20th, was spent in "clothing and painting" the engine, and the normal service was resumed the following day. Greatly increased efficiency in the working of the engine was reported, the running costs per ton-mile being only $\frac{5}{8}$d as compared with $\frac{7}{8}$d (£1 18s per day) previously. In sharp contrast the cost of horse power was $1\frac{1}{2}$d per ton-mile; it must be realized that the horse was able to haul less in a day than the steam engine – an indication of the value of steam engines on even so small a line if there was adequate traffic.

At the Annual General Meeting in May 1835 doubts were expressed as to the ability to supply all the sand required by the local farmers, despite a daily mileage exceeding 40 being performed on five days a week. The sand traffic had proved to be very lucrative, receipts for the period 4th July 1834 to 25th March 1835 totalling £408 12s 5d. Of this £206 1s 0d had been spent in purchasing the sand (the Company bought the sand at Wadebridge and resold it to the farmers) and with sand worth £5 in hand at the wharves a surplus of £207 11s 5d. was shown. Receipts from the carriage of passengers totalled only £23 12s 4d; this was never a very important source of revenue whilst the line remained isolated from the main network of British railways. An overall working surplus of £84 3s 10d was shown for the period of nearly nine months. This included a sum of £3 11s 6d in respect of fines imposed against trespassers. A second Act of Parliament was obtained on 30th July 1835, authorising additional capital of £5,000 and alteration to the Ruthern Bridge branch and to the wharves at Wadebridge and Bodmin. The total cost of the railway including the two Acts of Parliament, two engines and forty wagons amounted to £35,498 2s 9d, or about £2,450 per mile. This was a very low figure, and was in part due to some of the line being laid on Sir William Molesworth's property, which would have been sold to the company for a nominal sum. The upwards traffic consisted mainly of sea sand and some estuary mud for manure and coal, and was much greater than the downwards traffic, mainly minerals, of which the most important were tin and iron from Ruthern Bridge; copper, iron, tin and lead from Nanstallon; copper and iron pyrites from Wenford Bridge, from where granite from the de Lank Quarries was also forwarded. Parcels traffic was very spasmodic.

At a directors' meeting on 27th May 1835 the rate for conveying raw materials for export was reduced by over half to 1¾d per ton per mile. At the next meeting Mr Dunston reported that difficulty had arisen in the manufacture of new locomotive wheels and that it would be necessary to order these from the makers in South Wales. He also recommended that warehouses, in charge of a resident wharfinger, be built at Bodmin and Wadebridge for storing perishables and livestock, and was duly authorised to select suitable sites.

Camel started giving more wheel trouble on 2nd June; this continued into July, culminating on the 31st in having to leave the train at Dunmeer and return to the "house" (shed). On the 4th August "in returning from Wenford the engine wheel broke, obliged to put out the fire and bring it to Wadebridge with horses". On the 13th the whole of the spokes broke, and a connecting rod pin again broke on the 29th. To cope with the sand traffic it was necessary to work the Ruthern and Bodmin branches with horses. A proposal for obtaining a second engine, similar to *Camel*, but with larger cylinders, was considered at the same time.

Although there were public sidings, or "wharves", for the purpose, the obliging company was prepared to stop the train anywhere en route so that goods would be loaded or unloaded. In this way sand could be delivered to the field in which it was needed. Although this was very convenient for the farmers, it must have proved a source of considerable delay to the company. If goods unloaded from the train were not removed from the track within an hour a fine of £5 was imposed for each successive hour. On 16th October 1835 it was discovered that the engine's wheels were of different sizes "which shook the engine so much as to break a spring" and the Neath Abbey Company were asked to supply replacements; after these had been fitted the wheel trouble disappeared.

The replacement of firebars at very frequent intervals caused concern, and a test of fuel consumption was made, using various kinds of coal and coke. The daily figures were:

	Coal			Coke			
	t.	c.	q.	t.	c.	q.	
5th Nov. 1835		4	2	1	7	2	
4th Nov. 1835		6	0	1	7	2	
7th Nov. 1835	1	11	0	–	–	–	Tredegar coal
10th Nov. 1835	1	14	0		4	0	Liverpool coal

WADEBRIDGE IN THE 1880s

Above: the level crossing in the town centre, with the B&W office, surmounted by a clock tower, to the right and sailing ships tied up at the quay.
Below: looking across the Camel to Egloshayle with the lifting bridge raised on the sand dock siding.

Bodmin Wharf. A scene dating from sometime between 1886 and 1895 with the town omnibus Industry and open wagons bearing B&W and LSWR numbers. Since the frontispiece photograph was taken the sand drops have been filled in.

On the 7th November there was a slight mishap: "Used 31 cwt 2 qrs of coal from Tredegar. N.B. The road opened by which the engine and wagons went down between and caused a delay of two hours consuming 3 cwt of coal." *Camel* subsequently received a new, shorter, chimney ("stack") on 1st December to reduce the draught and the excessive burning out of the firebars.

At the half-yearly meeting it was stated that it was hoped to convey additional granite for the Great Western and other railway companies, for shipment from Wadebridge. The net profit for the half-year ending on 29th September had been £613 3s 7d, "or equivalent to about 4%." 13,514 tons of sand had been carried, and 2,320 passengers, who yielded £64 4s 6d. At this time there were ten barges, controlled by the Superintendent at Wadebridge, engaged in collecting sand from the Camel. The barges held 12 tons and for a full load a bargeman was paid 6s. At the end of the year applications were received to act as agents for the selling of sand at Helland and Nanstallon. The agents agreed to buy all the sand required at each depot and were paid a commission on sale. In February 1836 it was decided to let space for warehouses at Bodmin and Wadebridge, as the company was not prepared to undertake the work. The severe winter of 1835-6 affected the line; on 13th January 1836 the engine was unable to go out as the snow had frozen in the night. The sidings were completely full by the 15th February as farmers were unable to collect their sand, and traffic was suspended. The locomotive staff assisted the "blocklayers" (platelayers) on the track, or helped repair the fences, clear coal from the barges and other minor tasks. The engine worked only nine times in March, carrying about 38 tons upwards per trip. Activity in the local mines and quarries was at a low ebb, an average of only one ton per trip being carried back to Wadebridge.

Later that month the directors pledged their support for the London, Salisbury, Exeter & Falmouth Railway, doubtless hoping that their little system might become part of the trunk route from London to the then important trans-Atlantic port of Falmouth. In fact it was to be over fifty years before the line was connected to the main railway network, and even then not to its owners' lines. This was not due to a lack of support for other schemes, the little line soon finding that the effects of competition for the sand trade made serious inroads on the receipts. Some reductions in tolls were made, while representations were also made to Sir William Molesworth for reductions in the port dues at Wadebridge. On Sunday 15th May the sailing ship *Sophia* arrived at Wadebridge bringing the second engine, *Elephant*. The following day was spent in preparing for her disembarkation and on the 17th "all hands engaged in getting the Engine on shore from the *Sophia* – at 7 o'clock got the *Elephant* on Shore without any accident or injury." The first trial trip was on 6th June and the following week was spent in completing *Elephant* and cleaning *Camel*. The B&W was a pioneer operator of excursion trains and on the 14th June both engines were out, and two trains carrying between them nearly 800 passengers were run from Wadebridge to Wenford Bridge. The *Elephant's* train consisted of the omnibus, cab and seventeen wagons, and *Camel* followed with fourteen wagons. *Camel* had previously left Wadebridge at 5 a.m. with twenty-six wagons of sand, etc., for the various depots. The receipts at 1s each were £35 1s 0d. However *Elephant* soon began to give trouble, on 24th June "several pieces of granite fell off the wagons which occasioned much delay and consumption of steam which caused the lead rivet to melt – obliged to take out the fire and bring the engine home with cattle." She was very prone to leaking and by the 19th July had been laid up, and a strong complaint was made to the Neath Abbey Iron Works about her condition.

Camel was also in trouble for on 30th July "After passing Boro' Bounds (Dunmere) the Gibbs (sic) of the Sweep Rod of the Bell Crank broke which occasioned the separation (sic) of the Geer (sic) by which the Piston being forced to the bottom of the Cylinder with great violence, the Cylinder was fractured so as to allow steam to escape. Obliged to detach the Geer, and after taking the sand back to Boro' Bounds, the engine was worked home by hand." On the 9th September it had to be hauled back to Wadebridge by horses (not the only time this occurred) and during the night caught fire, but this was extinguished without much damage being caused. In September 1836 Mr Jordan, Senior, arrived from Neath to undertake a thorough overhaul of the *Elephant*. The repairs took a long time and it was not until 3 p.m. on 28th November that *Elephant* was "got out of the house", whence it proceeded with a truck of coal, and eight of sand, for Nanstallon. However it got no further than Pendavey when darkness fell and rough weather made it necessary to return. The square joint at the smokebox end, which had been causing trouble, was leaking very little. The journey was again attempted at 6.30 the following morning and went without undue incident but on returning the engine was detained "owing to the tide rising to an unusual height, the weather being exceedingly boisterous." After the engine had been put to "house" it was found that the leak increased as she cooled and Mr Jordan decided to make a new joint. The 6th December was spent in clothing the *Elephant* and examining pistons, etc.; the joint "that had given so much annoyance and occasioned so much expence and inconvenience appears to be cured by riviting (sic) the parts in lieu of a cement joint." Attention was then turned to *Camel*, and later in the month Mr

Jordan and his "attendants" were giving it a thorough repair. On 7th March 1837 it was tried without a load, and appearing to be all right took the train the following day as far as Grogley.

A long drought in May caused the engines to be stopped after Denby's and Shell woods had been set on fire on the 22nd, and horses were used for the rest of the week. On 14th June there was an excursion to Wenford similar to that run the previous year: *Camel* left Wadebridge at 5 a.m. with goods traffic for Wenford, and *Elephant* left at 7 a.m. for Bodmin. Both returned at 10.15 and the excursion left at 11, double-headed and composed of 27 vehicles carrying about 400 passengers. *Camel* returned to Wadebridge at 7.30 p.m. and *Elephant* at 10 p.m. Receipts were £26 11s 6d. These excursions must have seriously strained the resources of the company to provide the necessary rolling stock, there being at this time only two coaches and forty wagons. On the 7th September *Camel* was overturned in returning from Wenford when the flaunch of one of the wheels of the feeder broke. The following day was spent in rerailing; the tender was "injured", though the engine itself suffered no damage.

The "omnibus" could be hired by parties when not otherwise needed, the cost being raised from £2 2s to £2 10s in 1837, except that the cost would be £1 6s if there were under eighteen passengers. In October 1837 the Rev. William Molesworth was permitted to hire with the use of a horse for £3 for a day.

Towards the end of the decade the affairs of the company settled down somewhat, although the demand for sand dropped further, and by the early 1840s working losses of up to £200 per half-year were reported. In 1844, as an additional inducement, it was decided to let customers at Wenford Bridge have the exclusive use of "openings" (in the sand drops) if their traffic exceeded 20 wagon loads per annum. In the following year the Rock & Delabole Railway was proposed between those two points to convey traffic from the great slate quarry at Delabole to a new harbour at Rock, a small village on the Camel estuary opposite Padstow, but after a meeting with the B&W directors it was agreed to construct the new line from an end-on junction at Wenford Bridge up the valley of the River Camel to Delabole. Every facility was offered to the new company, an engine being placed at the directors' disposal so that they might inspect the Wenford line. By this time the B&W directors were trying any possible means of attracting new traffic, as the mines gradually closed and downwards traffic became virtually non-existent. Unfortunately they were largely unsuccessful, nothing more being heard of the Rock & Delabole Railway. On 2nd May the staff had to suffer salary decreases: the clerk, Preston Wallis, had a reduction from £50 to £37 18s 0d; the engineer from £104 to £94; whilst the carpenter faced the biggest cut, of over 50% – from £39 to £19. Owing to "the state of traffic and road" the engines were only being employed on the passenger service running on Saturdays and Fair Days, unless there was coal traffic to convey. On the other days horses were used, and the public were even allowed to use their own horses on payment of a toll. 911 barge loads of 12 tons of sand were unloaded at Wadebridge during 1844.

Chapter Three
Battle of the Gauges

At the half-yearly meeting in November 1844 it was resolved to try to connect with any "main trunk" railway nearby. By this time two such railways were considering plans for lines in the area. The Cornwall Railway proposed a broad-gauge line from Plymouth, where it would connect with the South Devon Railway and therefore the Great Western Railway, to Truro and passing nearly four miles southeast of Bodmin with a short branch to serve the town, whilst the standard gauge Cornwall & Devon Central Railway proposed a route from Falmouth through Wadebridge to Exeter, where connection with the London & South Western Railway was envisaged. Both of these companies offered to purchase the Bodmin & Wadebridge. The Cornwall made the first offer, a condition being that that company obtained its statutory Act of Parliament. An Extraordinary General Meeting was called by the board of the B&WR for 23rd October 1845, when the Cornwall Railway offer was announced. The meeting was adjourned *sine die* and meanwhile the Cornwall & Devon Central put in an unconditional offer for the B&W, which, although not as good as that of the Cornwall Railway, the B&WR directors wisely decided to accept, doubtless because firstly the offer did not depend on the company obtaining its Act, and secondly there was the possibility that the B&W would become part of a main line, and not remain a short branch-line.

The bill for the Cornwall & Devon Central was thrown out of the House of Lords in the 1845 session, but with active backing from the LSWR returned in the 1846 session, only to have the new bill rejected for not complying with Standing Orders. The negotiations for the purchase of the B&W were still incomplete, and with the failure of the Cornwall & Devon Central the LSWR stepped in and took over that company's responsibilities. At the time it appears to have been overlooked, or conveniently forgotten, that Parliamentary permission for the purchase had not been obtained, the first steps to remedy the situation not being taken until 1883. The purchase by the LSWR was a purely tactical move, designed to keep the Cornwall Railway and the broad gauge out of Wadebridge and North Cornwall. At the time the nearest point served by the LSWR was Dorchester, 120 miles east, although an extension from there to Exeter was envisaged. The LSWR replaced the B&WR shares with its own, and thenceforward became responsible for appointing the directors and staff. However there was very little local evidence of change and the railway continued much as it had done in the past; Mr Dunston remained as Superintendent at Wadebridge.

In September 1852 the LSWR sent the 0-4-2 goods engine *Atlas* to Wadebridge to replace the worn out *Camel* but by 1854 there was only one engine on the road, *Elephant* too being worn out, and the directors pressed the LSWR for a lighter engine and a more convenient carriage. Another 0-4-2 goods engine, *Pluto*, and two composite carriages were sent. These were used for a few years, but in 1861 Mr Hayes Kyd, who had come from Waterloo to succeed Mr Dunston as Superintendent in 1858, wrote to Mr J. H. Beattie, the LSWR Locomotive Superintendent, asking for a new engine; as a temporary measure it was decided to use horses for the time being. In 1862 it was agreed that china clay should be conveyed on the line; a century later it provided the majority of the traffic on the Wenford line and was the sole reason for its continued operation. A proposal that the Ruthern Bridge branch be extended to serve a projected iron mine at Withiel was rejected as being too risky although the company were prepared to work the line if the promoters constructed it themselves. By 1862 the directors' meetings were being held in the LSWR offices at Waterloo Bridge station in place of Bodmin.

In 1864 Joseph Beattie informed the board that the new engine recently supplied (an 0-4-0 saddle tank named *Bodmin*) could not be used unless repairs were made to the road. It was decided therefore to apply for powers to raise an additional £100,000 to rebuild the line. The whole amount was subscribed by the LSWR. The authorizing Act received the Royal Assent on 5th July 1865. Secondhand rails from the LSWR were used in the reconstruction of the Bodmin to Wadebridge section, the old rails from that section being utilised on the Wenford line. Some new rails were provided by the Rhymney Iron Co. in exchange for old rails. A further relaying proved necessary in 1879, when Vignoles rails on transverse wooden sleepers replaced the older form of track except on part of the Bodmin branch.

After the failure of the Cornwall & Devon Central Railway in 1846 there was considerable pressure in Cornwall for a standard gauge rival to the broad gauge group. However it was not until 1864 that the Launceston, Bodmin & Wadebridge Junction Railway obtained an Act of Parliament authorising the construction of a line from Launceston to Wenford Bridge, with running powers over the B&W. A further Act obtained the following year authorised an additional line southwards from

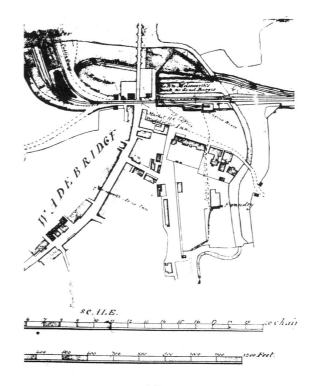

16

Ruthern Bridge to Truro, and a change of name to the Central Cornwall Railway. However it proved impossible to raise the necessary finance, and the powers lapsed in 1870. The B&W Act of 1865 contained permission to realign the Wenford line (involving several crossings of the River Camel) and the junction at Dunmere, and construction of a south to east curve near Grogley to accommodate through traffic, but nothing was done at the time. Subsequently the Devon & Cornwall Railway applied for powers to construct a line from its authorised Coleford Junction to Lydford line at Meldon to Wenford via Holsworthy and Jacobstow, with branches from Holsworthy to Bude, and Jacobstow to Launceston, where connection would be made with the Launceston & South Devon Railway. However only the Meldon to Holsworthy section was actually constructed at the time.

The Cornwall Railway had not exercised the powers for a Bodmin branch which it had obtained in 1846, and the nearest mainline station to the town was Bodmin Road, at Glynn Mill, nearly four miles away. In an attempt to remedy this the Bodmin & Cornwall Junction Railway was authorised by an Act of 4th July 1864 to construct the necessary link. On 2nd June 1865 additional powers were obtained, authorising an extension from Bodmin to join the B&W at Boscarne Mill. The B&CJR would naturally have been broad gauge and a break of gauge would have been involved at Boscarne Mill as the bill contained no proposals for changing the gauge of the B&W. The company suffered the same fate as so many of the period, being unable to raise the capital, and did not undertake any construction. It lingered on until 1880, when it was wound up.

Two lines proposed in 1873 were of local interest, and were under identical control. The Bodmin & Wadebridge and Delabole Railway was yet another attempt to provide a rail connection from Wenford to the great slate quarry at Delabole, whilst the Cornwall Minerals and Bodmin & Wadebridge Junction Railway was to connect the Cornwall Minerals Railway, then under construction from Fowey to Newquay, with Ruthern Bridge. The object was to provide an outlet for mineral traffic superior to Wadebridge. The two lines were granted running powers between Ruthern and Wenford, construction of a direct curve at Grogley to avoid a reversal there was envisaged. Although authorised on 5th August 1873, no construction was undertaken owing to the failure of a mining company which had guaranteed a considerable amount of traffic, and despite an extension of time being granted in 1876 the companies were wound up by Acts of 28th March 1878.

After the Bodmin & Cornwall Junction Railway had been wound up in 1880, the GWR obtained new powers for a standard gauge line over a similar route. Subsequently on 18th August 1882 the North Cornwall Railway, with the backing of the LSWR, obtained an Act for a line from Launceston to Wadebridge and Padstow. This Act included powers to reconstruct the B&WR between Wadebridge and Boscarne to accommodate GWR trains. These were transferred to the LSWR by that company's Act of 20th August 1883, which also sought to legalise its ownership of the B&WR, but opposition from the GWR was encountered and this was dropped. An agreement was drawn up in 1886 between the LSWR, B&WR and GWR to control the access by the latter to Wadebridge. The LSWR was to reconstruct the B&W, and construct a new station at Wadebridge; the GWR were to be permitted to appoint booking and invoicing clerks and an inspector, and were to re-imburse the LSWR the cost of other staff. The LSWR legalized its ownership of the B&WR on 1st July 1886, the Act receiving the Royal Assent on 25th June. The reconstruction commenced in 1886 and included deviations near Grogley, where there was a sharp curve, and Dunmere Junction, and provision of the new station at Wadebridge. The cost of the work was £15,118.

The B&WR passenger service was suspended from 1st November 1886 to enable the new works to be completed as soon as possible; the goods service was later suspended intermittently. The GWR opened its branch from Bodmin Road to Bodmin on 27th May 1887, and the extension thence to Boscarne on 3rd September 1888. Thus after 54 years the B&WR was at last connected to the main railway network, but not however to its owners' lines. Until the abolition of the broad gauge in 1892 there was break of gauge at Bodmin Road. The LSWR obtained an Act on 21st July 1891 to reconstruct the Bodmin branch beyond Dunmere Junction; a new course was followed for some three-quarters of a mile to eliminate the level crossing with the main road, which is on a steep hill, and to ease the steep gradients. Even so, parts of the line were still at 1 in 40.

Mr Hayes Kyd had retired in 1888 after 30 years service. After retirement he lived in Wadebridge until his death on 15th December 1891. He was buried in St Breock Parish Church, Wadebridge, where his tombstone records his association with the railway. He is remembered particularly for the many pints of cocoa and ale that he authorised for consumption by his staff at the railway's expense in lieu of overtime payment! As Superintendent at Wadebridge he was not only responsible for the day to day running of the railway, but acted as shipping agent on behalf of the mines, etc.

A notable character who had a long association with the line was one Samuel Worth, born in St Mabyn in 1815. He joined the railway upon its opening as a look-out man, on the front of the engine; his duties included opening and closing gates, warning the driver to stop if there were passengers to pick up, and chasing cattle from the line. He was later promoted to fireman but was seriously injured in a shunting mishap at Helland in 1835. On returning to duty in 1837 he was appointed wharfinger at Bodmin, and remained in charge there until 1895, when he retired at the age of eighty! On the occasion of a visit by the LSW Directors in 1886 he had caused the following notice to be posted outside Bodmin station: "Trains will not run today as the Directors are coming."

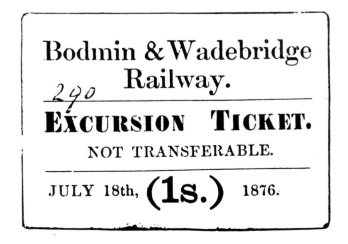

Bodmin & Wadebridge Railway.

290

EXCURSION TICKET.

NOT TRANSFERABLE.

JULY 18th, (1s.) 1876.

Chapter Four
The LSWR arrives in Wadebridge

The re-introduction of passenger services between Wadebridge and Bodmin (LSWR) took place on 1st November 1895, five months after the opening of the Delabole to Wadebridge section of the North Cornwall Railway on 1st June. The B&W was thus finally connected to its parent system. The North Cornwall's extension to Padstow was opened on 27th March 1899. When the passenger service to Bodmin was reinstated in 1895, the old practice of stopping anywhere en route was abandoned, and thus there were no intermediate stopping places on the 6¾ mile journey. Steam rail-motor cars were introduced on 1st June 1906, and on 2nd July three halts were opened, at Grogley, Nanstallon and Dunmere. None served any large population. Only LSWR cars called at the halts; Grogley was unlit, and was served in daylight only. In 1902, and again in 1912, the LSWR investigated the possibility of introducing passenger services on the Wenford line, and plans for re-aligning some of the sharper curves were prepared. A steam railcar made a trial trip in 1912, but stuck on one of the curves, and had to be rescued by a Beattie Well-tank. It was, however, felt that the expenditure necessary could not be justified, in view of the poor return that would result.

After the turn of the century the line had an uneventful existence. Ten years after the Southern Railway had absorbed the LSWR in 1923, the Ruthern Bridge branch was closed on 30th December 1933; the last train had run on 29th November. For some time the line had been used only occasionally, for agricultural traffic, the local mines having closed many years earlier. The last of the once extensive sand traffic was carried in the 1920s. The Centenary of the B&WR in September 1934 was celebrated by an Exhibition of relics held at Wadebridge Town Hall on 5th and 6th; on the 5th a special commemorative train was run from Wadebridge to Bodmin and back, headed by "O2" class 0-4-4 tank No. 216.

During the Second World War the section from Boscarne Junction to Wadebridge was upgraded to permit important GWR trains from West Cornwall to use the SR route to Exeter should their own route via Plymouth have been blocked by German bombing of that city. This route, involving four reversals (at Bodmin Road, Bodmin, Wadebridge and Exeter St David's) was only used on a few occasions but was revived for a period in the winter of 1960 for freight and milk trains when the Royal Albert Bridge at Saltash was closed on Sundays for maintenance work.

After Nationalization in 1948 the line automatically became part of the Southern Region of British Railways, but was transferred for commercial purposes, with all the ex-Southern Railway lines west of Exeter, to the Western Region on 2nd April 1950, but reverted to the Southern in 1958. From 26th September 1949 the SR station at Bodmin was designated "North" and the ex GW station "General" to avoid confusion. In 1955 the WR produced a comprehensive plan for rationalising services in the West of England which was only partially carried out; this envisaged withdrawal of passenger trains on the B&W section, though retaining Bodmin

19

North and Wenford for freight traffic. In September 1962 it was announced that once again the Southern lines would be transferred to the WR, this time for all purposes, with effect from 1st January 1963.

There was little immediate outward difference but by 1964 the heavy hand of the Western Region had begun to make itself felt and an air of decay soon set in. In June of that year the Bodmin North passenger service was altered to become a shuttle to a new platform at Boscarne which cannot have achieved any worthwhile economy but caused severe inconvenience and drove away most of the remaining passengers. By this time closure was being mooted. The North Cornwall line was closed completely between Meldon Junction and Wadebridge as from Monday 3rd October 1966 and all passenger services were withdrawn between Bodmin Road, Bodmin General, Wadebridge and Padstow, and between Boscarne Junction and Bodmin North, with effect from Monday 30th January 1967.

The only sections remaining open for freight traffic were Bodmin Road to Wadebridge for "station to station" full truck load traffic and Boscarne Junction to Wenford for private siding traffic from the clay works. A notable and unusually enterprising initiative during June 1966 was the running of several public excursions from Wadebridge to Wenford using brake vans to commemorate the running of the first such train in June 1836. Wadebridge disappeared from the railway map in September 1978 when the freight service was withdrawn and the last trains were two special diesel multiple unit excursions on 17th December of that year organised by Bodmin Round Table. After this the only remaining traffic was the clay from Wenford.

The end of the railway came on 3rd October 1983 with the loss of the clay traffic; output was declining whilst heavy expenditure in renewing both the track and wagons would have been inevitable to ensure a long term future. The trackbed now forms the Camel Trail for walkers and cyclists from Bodmin and Wenford to Wadebridge and on to Padstow. The GW branch still survives under the auspices of the Bodmin & Wenford Railway preservation scheme which operates regular passenger services during the summer season between Bodmin Road (now renamed Bodmin Parkway) and Bodmin General, and the track survives to Boscarne Junction. As its name implies, the preservation scheme was conceived with the intention of running trains through to Wenford and this may yet be possible. Ten years after closure, reopening the line for clay traffic is being seriously considered and this has approval from North Cornwall District Council despite inevitable objections from users of the Camel Trail who do not wish it to revert to being a railway! Output of clay from Wenford is higher than it was ten years ago and the local lanes are unsuitable for heavy lorries. Planning permission has been received for reinstating the track and an application for a Light Railway Order was submitted in 1992. It is considered that, with the aid of government grants for the transfer of freight from road to rail, reopening could be accomplished quickly.

The new station at Wadebridge in 1913, with a steam railcar departing towards Padstow.

A busy scene at Wadebridge in 1959, with No.30587 on pilot duties, West Country No.34033 Chard on an up North Cornwall train and No.30199 with a train for Bodmin North.

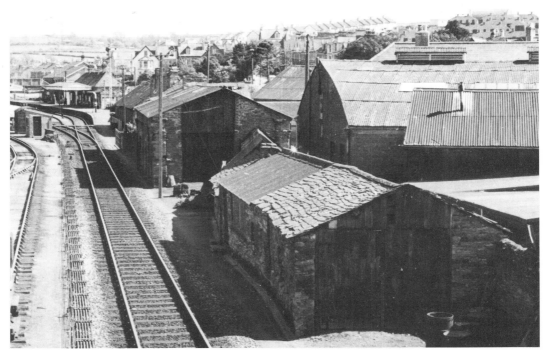

WADEBRIDGE

Top: A 1964 view from the West Signal Box with the B&W engine shed and workshop and the LSW station in the background.

Below: T9 No.30715 crossing the main road at the West box with a train for Padstow.

Chapter Five
Along the Line

WADEBRIDGE STATION

The B&W offices were situated to the east of the main road leading to the bridge across the River Camel. Although this was the official starting point of the B&WR a line continued west across the road to the quay, where in early days coal was brought in by ship, and stone and minerals formed return loads. A new single platform station with buildings constructed from local stone was built in 1888 to handle the GWR trains; it was enlarged with a new island platform in 1895 to handle North Cornwall line traffic and the Bodmin trains normally used the outer face of the island. The platforms were connected by an ornamental wooden footbridge which the SR replaced with a very narrow concrete structure. Until 1915 the GWR maintained a separate ticket office on the opposite side of the booking hall from that of the LSWR. Between the passenger station and the River Camel was the motive power depot with a two-road engine shed, coaling stage and 50ft diameter turntable; a line continued across the turntable to serve the old B&WR sand dock. The engine shed area was cleared in 1969, and the original B&W engine shed and workshops were demolished in the same year. There is now little trace of the railway in Wadebridge, the quay area has become an industrial estate whilst most of the station area has become a housing estate though the main station building has been carefully restored and is now the John Betjeman Centre for the retired, and the goods shed still survives nearby.

The Bodmin and North Cornwall lines left Wadebridge side-by-side, giving the appearance of double track although until 1906 there was only one line with a signalbox,"Wadebridge Junction", at the point where the routes diverged. After 1906 single line working commenced at the "East" signalbox, where there was formerly a siding to Guinea Port Quay. After the North Cornwall line swung away to the north the Bodmin line crossed the River Camel on Pendavey Bridge to enter the river's wooded valley. Shooting Range Platform (1 mile 40 chains from Wadebridge) was built in the 1880s to serve a nearby rifle range. It was used intermittently for many years (for example in 1909 LSWR Cars would call if not less than six volunteers wished to join or alight).

Although this part of the valley is subject to flooding the railway runs on the side of the valley, well above the river, and has not been badly affected, except in 1847 when the bridges at Dunmere and Grogley were swept away and Pendavey bridge severely damaged, and again on 27th October 1903 when Bodmin station was flooded to a depth of four feet after a cloudburst. Beyond Shooting Range Platform on the down side ("Down" was from Wadebridge to Bodmin) there was until 1930 a stone water tower, used to supply engines when the supply at Wadebridge was not available, a not infrequent occurrence in summer months.

GROGLEY AND THE RUTHERN BRIDGE BRANCH

About a quarter-mile before Grogley the old course of the line diverges to the south, behind the cutting through which the 1888 deviation ran. Although the connection at the western end was severed in 1888, the old line was used as a shunting neck to gain access to the Ruthern Bridge branch, a trailing connection with the main line at Grogley Halt (2 miles 72 chains) being controlled from Grogley Ground Frame. The branch, lifted in 1934, ran behind the halt at Grogley, crossed the river and ran southwards for over a mile to the goods depot at Ruthern Bridge (4 miles 6 chains). The original terminus had two sidings, one of which ran over sand drops; in 1914 a loop siding was installed 6 chains nearer Grogley, and in 1926 the branch was shortened by this distance and the old terminus removed. Although there was now a loop line the engine did not run round the train but propelled it back to Grogley, whence it proceeded to Boscarne. At the buffer stops at Ruthern Bridge the B&WR erected a stone mile post giving the exact distance from Wadebridge (4 miles 1 furlong 5 chains 10 yards); this distance was from the B&W station at Wadebridge, some 12 chains west of the LSWR one from which later mileages were measured. Similar posts were to be found every quarter mile and at the other termini. Midway along the branch a siding served an ochre pit, but even before the pit closed in 1912 the siding had been removed and wagons were left for loading on the running line.

The first Grogley Halt was a timber structure, the shelter being of the GWR "pagoda roof" type; it was replaced in 1957 by a standard concrete halt with a small concrete shelter. Access from the nearby lane is gained along the site of the Ruthern Bridge branch. The halt served a few isolated houses on the other side of the valley and was also used by anglers; the platform is still in place.

NANSTALLON, BOSCARNE AND DUNMERE
The line continued to climb through the valley beyond Grogley for over a mile. Immediately before Nanstallon Halt was Nanstallon Siding (closed 2nd May 1960) on the up side and facing down trains; it was usual for wagons to be detached from down trains and flyshunted into the siding. The small Nanstallon Signal Box was not a block post but controlled the level crossing with a minor lane; the Halt (4 miles 32 chains) is situated on the down side beyond the level crossing and could accommodate two carriages. The waiting shelter was of the "pagoda roof" type normally associated with the GWR but which was also found at the other halts on the line; the platform survives but part of the surface has been incorporated into the adjacent property. The lane to Nanstallon village and the bridge across the river were constructed by the railway company.

A short distance beyond Nanstallon is Boscarne Junction (4 miles 59 chains) where there was another level crossing. This was the end of the single line from Wadebridge East worked by Electric Tablet; the section to Bodmin North was worked by returnable electric Tablet, whilst to Bodmin General the GWR Electric Train Staff was used. All trains were required to stop dead to exchange tablets but this was in fact rarely observed.

The line then divided into four tracks, the southernmost line being the GWR line to Bodmin General. Between this and the SR line to Bodmin North was No.1 interchange siding in which traffic from the Southern was shunted to await collection by a WR train; similarly traffic from the WR was shunted into the northern siding (No.2). Thus Bodmin North trains ran between the two sidings. A connection between the running lines and the adjacent No.1 siding was also provided at the

WADEBRIDGE
Top: the heavily silted sand
dock with lifting bridge in
1934.

Centre: the shortened sand
dock siding in 1964, with
former London & North
Western Railway sleeping
car No.DM198932 which
was used as dormitory
accommodation for visiting
locomotive crews.

Below: the engine shed in
1962, with coaling stage to
right.

GROGLEY

Top: the view in 1933 from the platform end, looking towards Wadebridge. The 1895 deviation is to the right whilst the original route (centre) is a headshunt to reach the Ruthern Bridge branch on the left.

Centre: the second halt in 1964.

Below: Ruthern Bridge in 1926 with the minor road from Grogley alongside .

Ivatt class 2 tank engine No.41295 with the 2.52pm from Padstow to Bodmin near Grogley in May 1964.

east end of the yard, controlled from Boscarne Ground Frame. In May 1964 Boscarne Exchange Platform was erected in the vee of the junction; a normal height platform capable of accommodating a single unit diesel railcar was provided on the WR line and a short rail level platform on the Southern line. No.2 siding used to rejoin the Southern line just before it crossed the River Camel, the connection being controlled from Dunmere Junction Ground Frame, but latterly it ended in buffer stops. The only lines now remaining are the two tracks on the south side and an unconnected stub towards Dunmere. After the passenger services were withdrawn the signalbox was closed and the various lines to Bodmin General, Wadebridge and Wenford worked as sidings. Stop boards were erected to protect the level crossing and these still survive.

DUNMERE TO BODMIN

Immediately after the line crossed the River Camel the Wenford branch diverged at Dunmere Junction (5 miles 7 chains). The course of the original alignment of the Bodmin line can be seen first to the south and then to the north of the later route, rising alongside the Wenford line. The later alignment took the line on a right-handed curve on a rising gradient of 1 in 40 through a cutting past Dunmere Halt (similar to that at Nanstallon), situated on the main Bodmin to Wadebridge road. After passing under the road, the railway climbed through woodlands for over a mile until it passed Bodmin Gaol to arrive at Bodmin station (6 miles 51 chains). This was a

27

single platform station some distance from the town centre. The station buildings were of a neat single storeyed design of stone construction. There was a medium sized goods yard on the southern side. The single line section from Boscarne Junction was worked by Electric tablet; at Bodmin the instruments were housed in the station buildings. A single lever ground frame released the runround points.

Alongside the entrance to the goods yard could be seen the granite milepost erected by the B&WR reading "6 miles 7 furlongs 3 chains 8 yards". At one time it was preserved with a portion of the old track but in later years was allowed to decay; after the railway closed it was presented to the Bodmin Town Council and is now displayed in Bodmin Town Museum. A supermarket and its car park now cover most of the site.

THE WENFORD MINERAL LINE
After diverging from the Bodmin line at Dunmere Junction the line passed through a gate. Here the daily goods train waited for some twenty minutes whilst the guard or shunter returned to Boscarne Junction with the Electric Tablet for the section to Bodmin, without which he could not unlock the points at Dunmere. The Wenford line was worked "one engine in steam" without a train staff and was in effect a long siding. The SR Western Section Appendix dated 1960 stated that "Only one movement may be made on the line at one time. The line is not fenced and drivers must be prepared to stop short of any obstruction. Movements may be made only during daylight and a 20 ton freight brake van at least must be attached at the rear."

The line crossed the Bodmin to Wadebridge road at an ungated level crossing adjacent to which was Dunmere Siding (formerly Borough Bounds Wharf). The guard had to stop oncoming road traffic. As at several of the other level crossings on the line, the rails are still in place across the road complete with signs indicating an ungated crossing. The line was on a steep embankment alongside the river for much of the way; sharp curves abound and only four and eight wheeled goods stock was permitted. Over a mile from Dunmere Siding the site of Penhargard Siding, a loop used for loading timber, was passed; after a further three quarters of a mile steam trains stopped at Pencarrow water tank, fed by a nearby stream. Neither the Beattie well-tanks nor their successors, the ex GWR "1366" class, had sufficient tank capacity to make the complete journey from Wadebridge to Wenford and water was taken here in both directions.

The line emerged from the woods as it approached the site of Helland Wharf (8 miles 12 chains) closed on 2nd May 1960, where there was a siding facing down trains. The track squeezed between two cottages to cross a minor lane by another ungated crossing. Nearly 1¾ miles further on the site of the private siding which served the Road Stone Company's quarry at Tresarrett between 1911 and 1934 can be seen on the down side (9 miles 71 chains) and almost opposite on the up side, buried by trees and ivy, are the remains of the clay works formerly served by Parkyn's (Stump Oak) Siding (10 miles 0 chains). Shortly afterwards the line crossed another lane to reach Tresarrett Siding (10 miles 28 chains), another of the original "wharves" of 1834.

Exactly one mile from Tresarrett the line arrived at the china clay works of the English Clays Lovering Pochin & Co.Ltd (now English China Clays) which in the final years were responsible for all the traffic conveyed on the line. The clay, which is of a very high quality, is pumped from the mines on Stannon Moor, six miles away, to the works where it is dried and processed. Until 1967 the line continued beyond the works for nearly half-a-mile to arrive at Wenford Bridge (11 miles 63 chains), furthest point from Waterloo on the Southern Railway. The layout of the station was formerly similar to the original layout at Ruthern Bridge but in 1926 the yard was completely relaid to give a long run-round and two additional sidings. A five-ton overhead crane was also installed. One of the sidings continued across the road where it connected with the private tramway owned by the De Lank Quarries. This standard gauge line ran over the hill by means of a cable incline to the quarries, whence large quantities of granite were despatched by rail. Much of the stone used in the construction of London's bridges came from these quarries. The Quarry Company used a Simplex petrol shunter for working its sidings. The tramway was disused by 1950, but the abutments of the bridge that crossed the St Breward to Blisland road at the top of the incline can still be seen. The quarries are still active, and with the clay dries at Wenford are the last survivors of the mines and quarries that once supplied so much traffic to the railway.

A traveller in the brake van of the goods train in the late 1930s recorded* that it consisted solely of unbraked open mineral wagons, but there was also grain and animal feedstuffs traffic in covered vans to the wharves or sidings at Dunmere, Helland and Tresarrett which at that time were all in the hands of female wharfingers. At that time the clay from Wenford was sent to either Padstow or Fowey for shipment. Twenty years later some of the clay was bagged and this too was loaded into covered vans.

THE CAMEL TRAIL
The trail, created by Cornwall County Council and North Cornwall District Council, starts at Padstow station and runs along the trackbed of the railway through Wadebridge to Dunmere, where it divides for Bodmin and Wenford. It finishes about half a mile short of Bodmin North and at Poley's Bridge, opposite the entrance to the Wenford clay dries; there is no access between the clay dries and Wenford Bridge terminus, which is now a private coal yard. There are car parks at the principal points of access, which apart from the termini and Wadebridge include Grogley, Dunmere, Helland and Tresarrett though it should be noted that there is no public right of way for vehicles to Boscarne Junction. There are cycle hire shops in Padstow, Wadebridge and Bodmin, whilst the Western National rail replacement bus service from Bodmin Road (Parkway) to Padstow serves Bodmin, Dunmere and Wadebridge making it easy to walk this section in one direction and return by bus; the Wenford end can also be reached by buses from Bodmin to St.Breward on Mondays and Fridays. There is a tea garden in the grounds of a house at Nanstallon. It is noticeable that trees which have been allowed to grow since the demise of steam trains have made some parts of the trail more enclosed than they were thirty years ago. As the trail has not been dedicated as a public right of way the Dunmere to Wenford section could be closed if the plans to relay the railway succeed but through access from Bodmin to Wadebridge would be maintained as there is a parallel public path between Dunmere and Boscarne.

* article by C.E.Lee, Railway Magazine December 1940

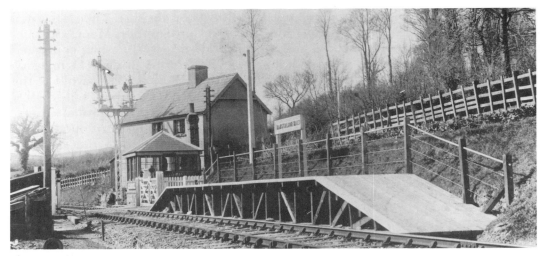

NANSTALLON
Top: the original halt when new with ground frame and Boscarne's splitting distance signals.

Centre: the rebuilt halt in 1962.

Well tank No.30585 arriving at Boscarne Junction with the Wadebridge to Wenford freight in September 1959.

BOSCARNE JUNCTION

Great Western 2-6-2 tank No.4585 with the 3.28pm Wadebridge to Bodmin Road passing No.30585 with the freight from Wenford in August 1954.
Below: the railbus from Bodmin North waiting at the newly built rail level halt in July 1964.

PANNIER TANKS AT DUNMERE JUNCTION

Top: No.1369 heads onto the Wenford line with a train of empty clay wagons in October 1963.
Below: the 57xx class had a short stay in the Wadebridge area, No.4666 (still sporting a Danygraig (Swansea) shedplate) heads for Bodmin North with a passenger train in July 1960.

BODMIN

Top: O2 class No. 30199 climbs the last few yards past Bodmin Gaol to arrive in the station in September 1961.
Below: Ivatt tank No. 41320 after arrival with a passenger train from Wadebridge in October 1963.

No.30585 heads across the main road at Dunmere with the Wenford train in June 1960.

**In the last year of steam operation a train of china clay heads away from Boscarne Junction towards Bodmin
General headed by N class No.31849 and banked by No.31840. May 1964.**

ON THE WENFORD LINE
Above: An idyllic scene in Dunmere Woods with No.30586 in May 1962.
Below: taking water at Pencarrow in August 1954.

The Tresarrett Quarry Company's stone crushing and loading plant, served by a narrow gauge line from the quarry on the far side of the River Camel. The Wenford line is out of sight in the foreground. The loading bank (right) still survives but the area is now thickly covered by trees.

No.30587 has arrived at Wenford Clay Works with the train from Wadebridge in September 1961.

A general view of the Clay Works at Wenford, looking towards Wenford Bridge, with No.1369 shunting wagons in October 1963.

The terminus at Wenford Bridge, with the goods office to the left, remains of the line to the De Lank Quarry in the foreground, and 5 ton hoist (right).

DE LANK QUARRY

Top: the top of the incline from Wenford Bridge, looking towards the quarry, with the bridge over the Blisland to St. Breward road in the foreground.
Below: A 1902 view of the quarry.

Chapter Six
Locomotives and Rolling Stock

EARLY LOCOMOTIVES

The original engine, the *Camel*, was built by the Neath Abbey Iron Works at a cost of £275. A contemporary report* records it as "mounted on six wheels of 3ft 9in diameter. Its weight is 11½ tons when working. The cylinders are 10½in diameter and the length of the stroke is 2ft. The working pressure of the steam is 50lb on the square inch." The engine had vertical cylinders and was painted black with yellow lining. In 1835 the directors of the railway decided that the traffic justified a further engine, and placed an order with the makers of the *Camel* for another similar engine, to be named *Elephant*. The specification for *Elephant* was for the "boiler shell to be 12ft long by 4ft 6in diameter, and resting on 8 standards fixed to a West Iron Framing to be suspended on four strong springs and four wheels with axle boxes. The fireplace and tubes to be constructed in the same manner as that of the locomotive engine *Hawk* of Harfords Davies & Co. of Ebbw Vale. The tubes to be of copper 2½in diameter, ⅛in thick and 18 to 20in long. The chimney to be 15in diameter and 2ft higher than on *Camel* to stop sparking (later altered to 13in diameter and 18in higher than *Camel*). The Cylinders to be 12½in diameter x 2ft stroke, to be placed vertically and the power to be conveyed to the wheels by Bow rods, bell cranks and cogged wheels. The exit steam pipes from the cylinders to pass through two heaters. Two feed pumps to be provided to supply the boiler, to be stronger than those of *Camel*. Two safety valves as before, one under the control of the engineer. The weight to exceed that of *Camel* by as little as possible." The new engine was not required to do more work than *Camel* but the larger cylinders were to enable it to perform the same duties "with less pressure and hazard." The cost was £820, less £40 allowed owing to trouble with *Camel*'s tubes; as the B&WR could not raise the money within 3 months of delivery £805 was offered and accepted for payment in six months.

The specification for *Elephant* quoted above contradicts the earlier report by implying that the engines were four coupled, not six coupled, and this is borne out by a report by Joseph Beattie, the LSWR Locomotive Superintendent, in September 1852, stating the *Camel* and *Elephant* ". . . have in the last few years been fitted with new wheels and springing. They are four coupled at present, but *Camel* is said to have been six coupled when new. The boilers and fireboxes have received repairs locally, quite efficient work, but more after the style of marine practice and tolerance than of railway practice of main-line companies. The safety valves are unreliable and care has to be taken by the men not to overfire these engines and strain the boilers. *Camel* is worn out and unsafe to work, *Elephant* is weak, but fully serviceable at present; mileage of boiler 209,632½." As replacement for *Camel* he arranged for the rebuilding of an old LSW 0-4-2 goods engine built in 1841 by Jones, Turner & Evans and named *Atlas*. The engine had 4ft 6ins coupled wheels,

*West Briton & Cornwall Advertiser, 17th October 1834.

and the rebuilding included new 14½ins x 20ins cylinders, a partially reconditioned firebox, new tubes, and a reconditioned tender. *Atlas* was shipped aboard
the sailing vessel *Stag* from Rotherhithe, and was at work on the B&WR before the
end of September 1852.

Following its arrival, *Camel* was laid up, but *Elephant* was given sufficient repairs
to permit its occasional use. However by 1854 it too was completely worn out and
Joseph Beattie was asked for a six coupled engine to replace it. However the B&W
foreman requested that if the extra engine were six wheeled it should be four coupled, as the permanent way couldn't bear a six coupled engine. With the success of
Atlas in mind, he suggested *Pluto,* a similar 0-4-2 goods engine, but built by Sharp
Roberts., which was working at the time as a stationary engine in the Nine Elms
Saw Mills. The engine entered shops in August 1854 for the fitting of 14ins x 20ins
cylinders, 5ft coupled wheels, a new copper firebox and a reconditioned 650 gal-
lon tender. Ready for service on 14th December, the weather was so severe that it
was not until March 1855 that *Pluto* and two composite carriages could be shipped
by sea to Wadebridge. From time to time spare parts were sent from Nine Elms for
repairs to be undertaken locally, but by the early 'sixties both were practically worn
out and quickly becoming too small for their daily work. Thus in February 1863 a
four-coupled saddle tank was ordered from Fletcher, Jennings & Co. of
Whitehaven. Named *Bodmin,* this engine arrived at Wadebridge in March 1864 and
replaced the LSWR 0-4-2s. In July 1865 the discarded engines were offered for sale
and on 23rd November were sold to a Mr Tregasse for £100. They were probably
only fit for scrap by this time. The original B&W engines, disused for over 10 years,
were sold to a local scrap dealer for £38 in October 1865.

At the end of 1873 *Bodmin* was in need of heavy repairs which could not be
undertaken locally. Thus in January 1874 the LSWR Locomotive Department
bought a 2-4-0 side tank named *Scott* from the Engineer's Department for £950.
Scott was built by George England in 1861; it had 11ins x 16ins outside cylinders
and 3ft 10ins coupled wheels. Following overhaul at Nine Elms it was sent by sea to
Wadebridge in March and *Bodmin* was returned to Nine Elms for attention. On the
latter's return it was decided to retain *Scott* at Wadebridge to assist at busy periods.
When *Bodmin* had to make another visit to Nine Elms in August 1885 an 0-6-0 sad-
dle-tank, No. 458 *Jumbo,* was sent as relief. Built by Manning Wardle in 1862, it had
been bought from J. T. Chappell for £650 in September 1883. When *Bodmin*
returned, *Jumbo* was retained and the smaller *Scott* was returned to the Engineer's
Department at Wimbledon in March 1886.

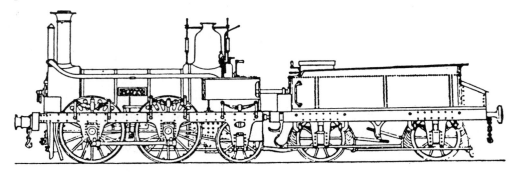

Pluto as rebuilt for the B&W line.

BODMIN & WADEBRIDGE MOTIVE POWER
Top: the Fletcher, Jennings 0-4-0 tank Bodmin.
Below: LSW No. 458 Jumbo.

A QUARTET OF BEATTIE WELL TANKS

Top: No.248 at Bodmin circa 1895. Apart from the addition of a cab the engine is virtually in original condition. Samuel Worth (sporting a fine beard) is standing in front of the engine.
Below: Southern Railway No.0314 (later BR No.30585) with Drummond boiler and Adams chimney, prior to its 1931 rebuild.

Top: The survivor with square splashers, Southern No.0329 (later BR No.30586) also photographed prior to being rebuilt in 1929.
Below: Southern No. 3298 after being rebuilt with new front end and steel buffer beam, and fitting of Drummond chimney.

ENGINES AFTER 1886

After the LSWR had legally absorbed the B&W in 1886, *Bodmin* and *Jumbo* were retained at Wadebridge. In May 1893 Beattie well-tank No.248 arrived by sea from Southampton, starting an association between the class and the B&W that was to last for sixty nine years. The well-tanks were designed by Joseph Beattie and built in large numbers from 1862 to 1875; originally they monopolised the extensive London suburban services of the LSWR but by the 1890s they were being displaced as the trains became longer and new locomotives took over. No.248 was one of the last to remain in its original condition; a cab was added during its stay at Wadebridge.

When the B&W was connected to its parent system with the opening of the North Cornwall line in 1895 *Jumbo* was returned to Exmouth Junction and its place taken by No.392 *Lady Portsmouth*, another Manning Wardle 0-6-0 saddle tank built in 1862; however it was inadequate for the traffic and soon returned east. Meanwhile *Bodmin* had been sold for scrap with the arrival of No.248 in 1893. Also in June 1895 rebuilt Beattie well-tank No.298 was sent to Wadebridge to replace No.248 and it was subsequently joined by Nos 314 and 329. The engines with their short wheelbase and light construction were ideal for the Wenford and Ruthern Bridge lines but by 1898 all the other eighty two of the class had been withdrawn and it was decided that they too should be scrapped in view of their poor condition. Adams "O2" 0-4-4 tank No.228 was sent for trial in September 1900 but soon proved to be unsuitable; "Ilfracombe Goods" 0-6-0 No. 301 was then sent to Wadebridge but did not venture onto the Wenford line and the inspector sent to supervise the trials recommended that the well-tanks should be repaired and retained. Thus after extensive overhaul they were returned to traffic. As withdrawal had been expected, their numbers had been allocated to new engines and so all three were placed on the Duplicate List, initially bearing a line drawn beneath the number and subsequently becoming Nos 0298, 0314 and 0329, being known as the "0298" class.

By 1920 they were again in need of heavy overhaul and they were all sent to Eastleigh works and fitted with new boilers during 1921. In the summer of 1928, after the LSWR had become one of the constituent companies of the Southern Railway, ex South Eastern & Chatham Railway "P" class 0-6-0 tank No.A558 was tried on the Wenford line together with ex Plymouth, Devonport & South Western Junction Railway 0-6-0 tank No.E756 *A. S. Harris* but neither proved suitable. The well-tanks again needed repairs and in August 1929 No.0329 was condemned but the lack of a suitable replacement led to yet another reprieve and between 1931 and 1935 all were rebuilt with steel leading buffer beams, new front ends to the frames and Drummond pattern chimneys. The Southern Railway initially prefixed LSWR locomotive numbers with the letter E (for Eastleigh, their 'home' works) to distinguish them from locomotives of its other constituents, but from 1931 the Duplicate List numbers had three thousand added so they now became Nos 3298, 3314 and 3329. Under British Railways they were again renumbered, becoming Nos 30587/5/6 respectively.

Nos 30585 and 30587 were built by Beyer Peacock of Gorton in Manchester in 1874; No.30586 was built the following year and was of a slightly different design with square splashers to the driving wheels. In their later years two were used at any one time – one working the Wenford freight, one acting as Wadebridge pilot and one spare. No.30586 was only used on the Wenford trip if the others were not available as it had a higher tank filler cap and took longer to replenish the tanks at Pencarrow. They also took a hand on passenger services right up to their withdrawal and were to be seen on trains of one to three coaches. This occurred quite frequently when the WR introduced diesel power on the services from Bodmin Road. On one occasion, 7th December 1961, following a collision at Bodmin General involving a pannier tank and the blocking of the North Cornwall line by a derailment, Nos 30585 and 30586 were used on the local Bodmin North and Padstow services all day.

They were finally superseded on regular services in August 1962 but No.30587 worked a farewell trip for railway enthusiasts to Wenford on 8th September 1962 and in December of that year made two trips together with No.30585 on the once familiar London suburban lines before withdrawal. No.30586 was scrapped but fortunately the others were preserved; No.30585 is at the Buckinghamshire Railway Centre at Quainton Road and No.30587 is part of the National Railway Museum collection and is at Buckfastleigh station on the Dart Valley line.

The replacements were three ex GWR outside cylinder 0-6-0 pannier tanks which had become part of the Southern Region's stock. Nos 1367-9 were members of the "1366" class introduced by C.B.Collett in 1934 and had been recently displaced at their previous haunt on Weymouth Quay by diesel shunters. No.1368 was tested in May 1962 but their general introduction had to await modification to the water tank at Pencarrow. However their stay at Wadebridge was short lived for after only two years they were replaced by Drewry diesel shunters. No.1369 had the privilege of hauling two farewell trains consisting of goods brake vans for enthusiasts to Wenford on 19th September and 31st October 1964 and has now been preserved for service on the Dart Valley branch.

Although the "O2" class 0-4-4 tanks were deemed unsuitable for the Wenford line they took over the passenger services in 1900 and operated for over sixty years. In British Railways days two were shedded at Wadebridge, for many years Nos 30200 and 30203. In later years they too were replaced by ex GWR pannier tanks. In 1960 pannier tanks Nos 4666 and 4694 were in use with No.30200 retained as spare engine but by the summer of 1961 No.30199 (destined to be the last survivor apart from those on the Isle of Wight) was being used. In 1962 the pannier tanks were in turn replaced by ex LMS Ivatt class 2 2-6-2 tanks; the last to be shedded at Wadebridge was No.41295 and amongst others used were No.41272 (the 7,000th engine built at Crewe), 41275 and 41320.

Adams "B4" class 0-4-0 tank No.99 was sent to Wadebridge in 1899 for use on shunting duties and the Bodmin goods but proved unpopular because of its small coal capacity and a tendency to derail in the sidings at Wadebridge and was returned in 1901. During the period from 1906 to 1918 many of the passenger workings were in the hands of Drummond steam rail motor cars, sometimes hauling a trailer. Railcar operation commenced on 1st June 1906, car No.13 being used alone until 14th June when No.14 arrived to assist. Later No.10 replaced No.13, probably after the latter's firebox split on 5th February 1907. In the summer months of 1913-14 the services were being worked by Nos 4 and 5 and in mid-1915 Nos 3,4 and 10 were in use. Although they were cheaper to run than a conventional train, maintenance was difficult; they had to be serviced in the engine shed which made it difficult to keep the carriage portion clean, and they were under-

ADAMS RADIAL TANK AT WADEBRIDGE

Top: Southern No.050 on shed.
Below: No.050 heads off to Bodmin, the single coach is a converted railmotor.

powered. Railcar operations ceased at Wadebridge in May 1918 bringing an end to their use on the LSWR.

An Adams "415" class 4-4-2 radial tank was shedded at Wadebridge after 1906 for working to Bodmin, primarily on goods and mixed trains. Apart from those retained for working the Lyme Regis branch No.050 of Wadebridge was one of the last survivors of the class being withdrawn in 1927, however No. 3125 was reportedly covering the Bodmin service at Whitsun 1947 when "O2" No.203 was away for repairs. In the last years of steam operation an "N" class 2-6-0 was diagrammed for the daily goods train to Bodmin between duties on the North Cornwall line and there was latterly also a morning passenger duty.

The Southern Region's Engine Route Availability book issued in 1954 listed the following classes as permitted to work over the Bodmin and Wadebridge section: "C14" (0-4-0T), "E1/R" (0-6-2T), "O2," "0395", "757", "0415", "0298", British Railways standard class 2 and 4 2-6-0, class 3 2-6-2T; the following classes were permitted at a maximum speed of 25mph: "N" and "U" 2-6-0, British Railways standard class 4 2-6-4T and ex-London, Midland & Scottish Railway class 4 2-6-0 and 2-6-4T. The next issue, dating from 1962 and destined to be the final SR issue covering the lines west of Exeter, additionally listed the "N1" and "U1" 2-6-0, "B4" and "T9" classes at a maximum speed of 25mph, "700" class 0-6-0 on snowplough duties only, ex-GWR "1366" and modified "57xx" classes, diesels of classes "D2000", "D8200", "D8400", "D63xx" (between Boscarne Junction and Wadebridge), "D70xx" (maximum speed 20mph) and electro-diesels E6001-6 . Some of these types never operated anywhere near Wadebridge and an anomaly is that the British Railways standard class 9 2-10-0 is shown as authorised to work between Boscarne Junction and Bodmin Road, despite being banned from working anywhere else on the SR west of Exeter, and on the Western Region west of Plymouth. The Southern listed the "O2" class as authorised to work through to Bodmin Road, and the "N" and "U" classes between Boscarne Junction and Bodmin General but made no reference to the Beattie welltanks, which seem to have worked to Bodmin General without authorisation, whilst the WR version makes no reference to ex-Southern classes.

From its opening the North Cornwall line trains were generally in the hands of various classes of Adams and Drummond 4-4-0s, though the "0395" 0-6-0s and "A12" or "Jubilee" 0-4-2s were also to be seen, whilst from the late 1920s Maunsell's "N" class 2-6-0s of South Eastern & Chatham Railway origin became common. In 1945 the Southern Railway introduced the "West Country" class of pacifics and the first twenty were all shedded at Exmouth Junction. Although they worked the heaviest expresses on the main line, they also appeared on the North Cornwall line. They could not be turned on the turntable at Wadebridge, which was of 50 ft diameter, and a new 65 ft turntable was installed at Padstow in 1947. They were named after towns on the SR, and appropriately Nos.21C107 *Wadebridge* and 21C108 *Padstow* were often to be seen. Special arrangements were made for No.21C116 *Bodmin* be taken to Bodmin North for a naming ceremony on 28th August 1946. During the British Railways era the "West Countries" shared duties with the "N" class and the "T9" class, last survivors of the LSWR 4-4-0s; the "T9s" lasted until 1961 apart from No.30120 which was preserved and made one final visit to Wadebridge in April 1963. There were also occasional appearances of "N1" and "U" class 2-6-0s. During the last months of steam operation in 1964 British Railways standard class 4 2-6-4 tank engines took over from the 2-6-0s and the "West

Countries" disappeared with the withdrawal of the "Atlantic Coast Express" in September 1964. Happily both *Wadebridge* and *Bodmin* were rescued from the cutters' torches; *Wadebridge* is now on the Bodmin & Wenford Railway and *Bodmin,* which was rebuilt in 1958 losing its air-smoothed casing, is on the Mid Hants Railway.

On the GWR branch from Bodmin Road the initial motive power was provided by 0-6-0 saddle tanks, Nos 1222 and 1224 being used at the opening. The saddle tanks of the essentially similar "850", "1901" and "2021" classes were gradually rebuilt as pannier tanks from 1910 onwards, and in this guise continued to work the line until in the 1920s they were superseded by the standard "45xx" 2-6-2 tanks which had virtually total command until 1962. Bodmin Road to Boscarne Junction was classified "blue" in the GWR system of route availability which meant that engines as big as the "Manor" 4-6-0 and "28xx" 2-8-0 classes could have been used . GWR engines working through to Wadebridge had to have their footsteps cut back to a maximum overall width of 8ft 4in. Apart from the "45xx" class and the "57xx" pannier tanks, in later years the only classes permitted to run to Wadebridge were the "2301" Dean goods and "2251" classes of 0-6-0, "43xx" class 2-6-0 and the large 2-6-2 tanks of the "51xx", "61xx" and "81xx" classes.

The "45xx" class was replaced by Type 2 diesel-hydraulic locomotives of the "D63xx" class in 1962 and thereafter the only steam engines seen on the Bodmin Road section were on Southern worked trains. With the commencement of the 1964 summer service the through Wadebridge-Bodmin North passenger service was withdrawn and replaced by an AC Cars four-wheeled diesel railbus running only to and from Boscarne Exchange Platform and the Bodmin Road-Wadebridge service was taken over by a single unit diesel railcar, with some railbus and diesel loco hauled workings. The Wenford and Bodmin North goods services were worked from August 1964 by a 204hp Drewry diesel shunter which was latterly superseded on the Wenford service by a British Railways 350hp diesel shunter from St.Blazey shed. In the final years a main line diesel locomotive, successively a "D70xx" Hymek, "D50xx" (class 25) and lastly "D67xx" (class 37) worked clay trains between Fowey and Boscarne Junction with the shunter operating between Boscarne and Wenford.

ROLLING STOCK

The B&WR originally provided two closed passenger vehicles, built locally. The first class carriage had three compartments and was 12ft long, 6ft wide and 7ft high, and weighed 2 tons. The second class carriage had two compartments, and was 9ft long and 6ft wide, seating 16 passengers. They were later superseded by the four carriages, two open and two closed, that have been preserved. The closed carriages had blue lower panels, white upper panels with crimson red underframes. The leather buffers were stuffed with horsehair. The composite coach had three compartments, the middle one being first class and the outer two were second class. The second class carriage had two compartments only; one of the third class "open" carriages had two, the other three, compartments. These had wooden buffers. The goods rolling stock at the opening consisted of 13 ore wagons, costing £13 each, and 27 wagons with bottom doors, for the conveyance of sand and coal, costing £30 each. For conveying granite blocks from the De Lank quarries the company later provided flat wagons. The goods stock was fitted with dumb buffers

The B&W passenger stock (left to right composite, second class & two open thirds) and a chauldron wagon.

and "pin & shackle" couplings. Few if any had brakes originally, but hand brakes were fitted on some later. The wheels ran loose on fixed axles. The LSWR sent additional stock in the 1880s; this bore the LSWR initials and was marked "B&W line", and carried both a LSW and a B&W number.

When the B&W Company was wound up in 1886 it owned the following stock:

2 tank engines	2 third class coaches
1 tender	137 wagons
1 composite coach	6 timber wagons
1 second class coach	3 guards' vans

The solitary tender was that of *Camel*, withdrawn over twenty years earlier. All four carriages are still in existence; prior to the Second World War two were displayed on the concourse at Waterloo station and all can now be seen at the National Railway Museum at York. Their origin is uncertain; although their design is from the early years of railways it is unlikely that any are the original vehicles and they were possibly built locally in the 1860s. However two composite carriages are recorded as being sent from the LSWR in 1855 and it is possible that one of these has survived.

After 1895 the line was worked with standard LSWR rolling stock. When the steam rail motor cars were withdrawn from traffic in 1918 the power units were withdrawn and the coaches used as trailers, some being fitted for push and pull operation. A one or two coach set of non push and pull fitted stock was used for many years on the Bodmin line, sometimes strengthened by an ordinary vehicle. The entrance to these cars was by means of a gated vestibule. Trains on the Bodmin line were described in the working timetable as being formed of rail motor cars well into the Southern era, long after the demise of the cars; passengers joining at the intermediate halts brought their tickets from the guards who were issued with specially printed sets of tickets. After nationalisation the converted rail motor cars were replaced, and until 1964 trains usually consisted of a "2 Set P", comprising a Southern Railway corridor brake/composite and a corridor brake/third carriage. In contrast the Western Region trains were formed of a two coach non-corridor "B" set.

SIXTY YEARS OF RAILCARS
Top: Drummond steam railmotor No.10 waiting to leave Padstow for Bodmin.
Below: AC Cars diesel railbus at Bodmin North in July 1964.

Chapter Seven
Train Services

EARLY DAYS

The first timetables provided for a passenger train from Wadebridge to Bodmin and back on Wednesdays and Saturdays, with a goods service on the other weekdays. However after a few years the sand traffic, upon which the line initially depended, declined and in the early 1840s receipts barely covered the working expenses. Thus economies proved desirable and as far as possible the goods service was horse drawn unless the coal traffic justified the use of the *Elephant* or *Camel*. In 1843 the Wednesday passenger train was altered to run on a Thursday and the only steam worked goods service ran on Tuesdays. In the next year the engines were being steamed only for the Saturday passenger train. The impending departure of a passenger train was announced by the blowing of the engine whistle ten, five and one minute before leaving.

The company was particularly fond of running special trains, there being a passenger service on all fair days and when the Assizes were sitting at Bodmin. On Tuesday 14th June 1836 it had run one of the first cheap public excursions when 800 persons were taken from Wadebridge to Wenford Bridge for the day in two trains; the 130th anniversary of this event was celebrated with the running of similar excursions consisting of a diesel shunter and goods brake vans. On 13th April 1840 an excursion was run from Wadebridge to see the public execution of the brothers William and James Lightfoot at Bodmin Gaol. So popular was this that three trains were run, conveying a total of 1,100 persons. The Bodmin Wharf adjoined the county gaol so the passengers did not have to leave the wagons, doubtless suitably cleaned for the occasion. According to an account in Bodmin Town Museum the double execution proved to be a big event, attracting thousands of sightseers.

After the LSWR assumed control in 1846 a daily passenger service was instituted but by the 1870s the Tuesday and Thursday services had been replaced by a goods train. On Mondays, Wednesdays and Fridays there was a morning service from Wadebridge, returning from Bodmin in the late afternoon. On Saturdays there were two return trips in the afternoon. Saturday was therefore the only day on which it was possible for Bodmin residents to visit Wadebridge, albeit briefly, and return on the same day. The service was frequently amended for special events, additional services being run for the Royal Cornwall Agricultural Society's exhibitions, cattle markets, flower shows and even local swimming matches and church bazaars. As previously mentioned, the service was suspended in 1886 to enable the railway to be reconstructed.

SERVICES 1895-1983

After the re-opening to passenger traffic in 1895, some eight trains per day were operated, one conveying a through carriage from Waterloo. The GWR provided six or seven trains to Bodmin (GW). The LSWR service was increased with the advent of the steam railcars in 1906. In the summer of 1909, for example, there were ten

Cars in each direction, one down LSWR mixed train conveying both passenger carriages and goods wagons (two on Saturdays) and one up LSWR passenger train. The GWR service consisted of five passenger and two mixed trains in each direction, with an additional return trip on Saturday evenings during July, August and September only. Only the LSW Cars to Bodmin served the halts, plus the 9.08am from Bodmin (LSW) on the second Tuesday in each month only (Wadebridge market day). No lamps were provided at Grogley and Cars only called during daylight. In addition to the mixed trains, the LSW ran a daily goods train from Wadebridge to Bodmin and back, and there were conditional pathways for an additional LSW trip from Wadebridge to Boscarne and back and for GWR trains from Bodmin (GW) to Boscarne or Wadebridge. A mineral train was run by the LSW to Wenford which served Ruthern Bridge when required on the outward journey.

In these days of constantly changing timetables it is worth recording that in the far flung outposts of Waterloo's empire little changed from year to year, and trains that ran in the 1920s were often identifiable right up to the early sixties. No regular Sunday service was ever operated but in the 1930s there was an excursion from Bodmin (SR) to Wadebridge on some three Sundays during the summer, connecting with a North Cornwall line excursion to Exeter and Paignton. The GW and LSW services normally operated independently but for a short time in 1919 an LSW train ran to Bodmin (GW) and in the summer of 1928 one GWR train was extended to Padstow. In Southern days there were several through workings between Bodmin and Padstow.

After nationalisation there was considerable interworking. In the summer of 1948 one Western Region train ran to Padstow, increased to two the following year. Also from the 1948 summer service the 8.10am from Padstow which formerly ran to Bodmin North (SR) was diverted to Bodmin General (WR) and starting in that winter's service the 8.02pm from Padstow was diverted to run through to Bodmin Road, replacing a Western Region train. There was little further change until June 1960 when two more trains were diverted away from Bodmin North, the 6.55am from Wadebridge running to Bodmin General and the 6.12pm from Wadebridge going through to Bodmin Road. By this time some of the Western Region trains were calling at Nanstallon Halt, and one at Grogley Halt. Until the withdrawal of loco-hauled passenger services mixed trains were scheduled to run on each line. There was also a daily goods train to Bodmin North, leaving Wadebridge at 1.02pm, returning at 2.15pm. The Wenford trip only ran on Mondays to Fridays, leaving Wadebridge at 9.35am and timed to arrive at Wenford at 12.41pm, returning at 1.20pm. The bulk of the china clay was exported via Fowey and was left in the exchange siding at Boscarne Junction for collection by a midday train from Bodmin General.

With the commencement of the 1964 summer timetable (but too late for inclusion in the public timetable) the service was radically altered and the Wadebridge-Bodmin North service replaced by a railbus from Bodmin North which terminated at the new halt at Boscarne Junction. The connecting services generally ran through between Bodmin Road and Padstow, most were single unit diesel railcars but some loco-hauled workings remained. At first there were only four trains to and from Bodmin North (five on summer Saturdays) but very soon an extra service from Bodmin at 5.50pm ran through to Wadebridge, replacing what had been intended to be an empty journey.

TRAINS TO THE GREAT WESTERN

Top: GWR No.4529 in early British Railways livery leaving Wadebridge for Bodmin Road in July 1949 with a standard 2-coach 'B' set.

Below: The Beattie welltanks made occasional forays onto Western metals; on Friday 13th July 1962 No.30585 is seen at a very wet Bodmin General with a single Bulleid corridor coach on what was possibly the last day it worked an ordinary passenger train.

STRANGE VISITORS

Top: A number of armoured trains patrolled the east and south coasts of England during the second world war but this view of former Great Eastern Railway 2-4-2 tank (possibly LNER No.7178) was taken at Wadebridge sometime in 1940 or 1941.

Below: Although the West Country Pacifics worked regularly on the North Cornwall line the only one to visit Bodmin was No.21C116, on the occasion of its naming on 28th August 1946.

In the summer of 1965 the situation improved slightly, with five arrivals and six departures at Bodmin North on Mondays to Fridays, and seven arrivals and nine departures on Saturdays. The railbus also worked round to Bodmin General to make two trips to Bodmin Road and back. During the week it was stabled overnight at Wadebridge, but on Saturday evenings it formed a passenger train from Wadebridge to Bodmin Road before continuing to St.Blazey depot for servicing. The goods workings were also revised to provide a through Bodmin Road to Wadebridge service, the locomotive then working the school train to Bodmin General. A diesel shunter was based at Wadebridge and this worked a freight to Bodmin North which returned to Boscarne Junction and then went to Wenford. On arrival back at Boscarne Junction conditional paths were provided for further trips to Bodmin North and Wenford if required before returning to Wadebridge. The North Cornwall line had been reduced to a local diesel multiple unit service running between Okehampton or Halwill and Wadebridge and the freight service withdrawn. On summer Saturdays the set of carriages used for the Bodmin school train was used all day between Bodmin Road and Padstow, providing with the regular diesel unit virtually an hourly service, probably the best ever operated; this entailed the trains crossing at Boscarne Junction giving rise to some complicated manoeuvres, especially as the Bodmin North railbus was there at the same time.

The published service from April 1966 showed a drastic curtailment of the service to Bodmin North. It was to be served by a mere two trains from Bodmin Road which on arrival at Boscarne Junction would have reversed to Bodmin North before continuing their journeys to Padstow. No return trains would have been run except on summer Saturdays when one train in each direction was planned. Presumably this scheme was abandoned because proposals for complete withdrawal of the passenger service had been published, and the 1965 timetable continued with minor changes until services ceased in January 1967.

It is worth noting that the Southern Region timetable of summer 1964 was the last to include the Bodmin service, coinciding with the end of through services from Waterloo to the North Cornwall line. During this period the Western Region published details of the Sunday omnibus service from Bodmin Road to Wadebridge and Padstow; after passenger trains were withdrawn Southern National provided a daily replacement service which was published in the railway timetable for many years. Unlike many other railway replacement services provided in the 'Beeching era' the service continues to flourish.

Bodmin and Wadebridge Railway.

No. *61* *Mch 3?* 188*8*.

Mr. *Collins*

Please to supply for the use of the BODMIN AND WADEBRIDGE RAILWAY,—

*1 Pint Cocoa to
E. Chudley ×*

*H. Hyd
Supt*

Order Check Book.—Liddell and Son, Printers, Bodmin.

APPENDIX ONE

Estimate by Rober Hopkins C.E. for constructing the railway from Bodmin to Wadebridge

An estimate of the Expence of Constructing an Iron Railway from Wadebridge in the Parish of St Breock to Bodmin in the Borough of Bodmin and to Wenford Bridge in the Parish of St Breward. Also of making to Branch Communications: the one to the Ruthern Bridge Road and the other to Nanstallon the whole being in the County of Cornwall as shewn on the map and section.

From Wadebridge to the Bodmin Turnpike Road near Dunmeer

Forming the road fifteen feet wide at top and on the inclination shewn on the section including all requisite cuttings and embankments and stoning under blocks well broken when required and making approaches to Roads and Fields when necessary 9732 yards lineal at 3/10	1865	6	0
Fencing on both sides of the road where necessary and providing and fixing Gates and Posts in the Fields through which the road will pass. 9732 yards lineal at 1/2	567	14	0
Making all requisite Culverts and Drains	80	0	0
Building a bridge across the new Channel at Wadebridge another across the River Camel near Pendavey and a third across the same river near Dunmeer	1440	0	0
Providing and laying stone Blocks each weighing at least 3 cwt and two to be laid in every yard in length 9732 yards at 2/-	973	4	0
Wrought iron Rails each weighing thirty five pounds per yard and cast iron pedestals each weighing ten pounds 391 tons at £7 10s including price at Newport Freight to Wadebridge Insurance and cartage to the Road	2932	10	0
Plugs Nails Pins and Cotters 9732 yards at 7d	283	17	0
Laying the Blocks and fixing the Pedestals and Rails on the Blocks and filling between the Blocks and Rails and on the outside of same with hard stone well broken and Gravelling the surface 9732 yards at 1/3	608	5	0
Engineers and Assistants laying out and Superintending the execution of the works, viz. Taking levels and laying out the Road by putting stakes in the ground to designate the bed of the road, and middle range, marking out the line of the Road on each side. Making specifications and estimates of the expences of the various works after the Road is laid out surveying and making such plans and sections as may be necessary for the execution of the works, particularly of the Bridges, giving directions for making the Iron Rails and Pedestals and the turnout plates and examining them when landed, levelling and putting stakes from time to time by which to lay the Blocks and Rails. Measuring and valuing the land required for making of the Road and general superintendence of the whole of the works as they proceed 9732 yards at 1/-d	486	12	0
Four turnouts 70 yards each. 280 yards at 12/-	168	0	0
Purchase of Land 22½ acres at £35	787	10	0
	£10192	**18**	**0**

From the Camel River between Pendavey and
Dunmeer to Bodmin

Forming including cutting, embanking, stoning under blocks and approaches. 2948 yards at 1/8	245	13	4
Fences Gates and Posts. 2948 yards at 1/3	184	5	0
Culverts and Drains	25	0	0
Stone Bocks. 2948 yards at 2/-	294	16	0
Rails and Pedestals. 118½ tons at £7 10s	888	15	0
Plugs, Nails, Pins and Cotters. 2948 yards at 7d	85	19	0
Laying the Blocks and Rails and filling with broken stone and Gravelling. 2948 yards at 1/3	184	5	0
Engineers and Assistants laying out and superintending the execution of the Works. 2948 yards at 1/-	147	8	0
2 Turnouts. 140 yards at 12/-	84	0	0
Purchase of land. 6½ acres at £50	325	0	0
	£2465	**2**	**0**

From the Turnpike Road near Dunmeer to Tresarrett Bridge

Forming including Cutting, Embanking, Stoning under blocks and approaches. 8816 yards at 1/10	808	2	8
Fences, Gates and Posts. 8816 yards at 1/2	514	5	4
Culverts and Drains	80	0	0
Stone Blocks. 8816 yards at 1/1	477	10	8
Rails and Pedestals. 354½ tons at £7 10s	2658	15	0
Plugs, Nails, Pins, Cotters. 8816 yards at 7d	257	2	8
Laying the Blocks and Rails and filling with broken stones and Gravelling 8816 yards at 1/3	551	0	0
Engineers and Assistants laying out and superintending the execution of the works. 8816 yards at 1/-	440	16	0
2 Turnouts 140 yards at 12/-	84	0	0
Purchase of land. 20 acres at £25	500	0	0
	£6371	**12**	**4**

From Tresarrett Bridge to Pawleys Bridge

Forming including Cutting, Embanking, Stoning under Blocks and approaches. 1371 yards at 2/2	148	10	6
Fences, Gates and Posts. 1371 yards at 1/3	85	13	3
Bridge over the Lank River and Culverts and Drains	130	0	0
Stone Blocks 1371 yards at 1/-	68	11	0
Rails and Pedestals 55 tons at £7 10s	412	10	0
Plugs, Nails, Pins and Cotters. 1371 yards at 7d	39	19	9
Laying the blocks and Rails filling between on and the outside of same with broken stone and Gravelling 1371 yards at 1/3	85	13	3
Engineers and Assistants laying out and superintending the execution of the works. 1371 yards at 1/-	68	11	0
1 Turnout 70 yards at 12/-	42	0	0
Purchase of Land. 3 acres at £40	120	0	0
	£1201	**8**	**9**

From Pawleys Bridge to Wenford Bridge

Forming including Cutting, Embanking, Stoning under Blocks and approaches. 1191 yards at 1/8	99	5	0
Fences, Gates and Posts. 1191 yards at 1/3	74	8	3
Culverts and Drains	10	0	0
Stone Blocks 1191 yards at 1/-	59	11	0
Rails and Pedestals. 48 tons at £7 10s	360	0	0
Plugs, Nails, Pins, Cotters. 1191 yards at 7d	34	14	9
Laying the Blocks and Rails and filling with broken stone and Gravelling. 1191 yards at 1/3	74	8	3
Engineers and Assistants laying out and superintending the execution of the Works. 1191 yards at 1/- ...	59	11	0
1 Turnout. 70 yards at 12/-	42	0	0
Purchase of Land 2½ acres at £35	87	10	0
	£901	**8**	**3**

Branch communications across the River and a cart road to join the Road leading to Ruthern Bridge	400	0	0
To Nanstallon	350	0	0
	£750	**0**	**0**

Grand Total: £21,882 9s 4d
Roger Hopkins,
Civil Engineer,
December 12th, 1831.

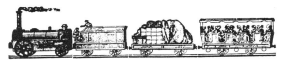

ATTENDANCE WILL BE GIVEN AT THE RAILWAY OFFICE,

ON THE WHARF AT BODMIN,

On WEDNESDAY, the 25th of January, 1871,

Also, on SATURDAY, the 28th of January, and SATURDAY, the 4th and 11th of February,

On each Day between the hours of Eleven and Five,

FOR THE PURPOSE OF RECEIVING

The AMOUNT due for SAND, on the 31st of December, 1870.

Any Accounts, not paid as above, may be settled at the OFFICE, at *Wadebridge*, on any day except the above, until the 13th of February, 1871. All Accounts, not settled on or before that day, will be handed over to the Law Clerk of the Company, and payment enforced without further notice, at the costs of the defaulters.

APPENDIX TWO

ARTICLES OF AGREEMENT made the Fifth day of June 1886 between the LONDON AND SOUTH WESTERN RAILWAY COMPANY (hereinafter called "The South Western Company") of the first part THE BODMIN AND WADEBRIDGE RAILWAY COMPANY (hereinafter called "The Wadebridge Company") of the second part and THE GREAT WESTERN RAILWAY COMPANY (hereinafter called "The Great Western Company", of the third part.

WHEREAS the Great Western Company by the Great Western Railway (No. 1) Act 1882 were authorised to construct a Railway from the Bodmin Road Station of the Cornwall Railway Company to Bodmin and to a point on the Bodmin and Wadebridge Railway near Boscarne Mill. And whereas by heads of agreement dated the 1st of October 1884 made between the South Western Company of the one part and the Great Western Company of the other part (hereinafter referred to as "The Agreement of 1884") it was provided that the Bodmin and Wadebridge Line should be considered a portion of the South Western System during the term of that Agreement or whenever the North Cornwall Railway joined it or after the Great Western Company's Bodmin Branch joined it if any arrangement was made between the Companies for the use of the Bodmin and Wadebridge Line by the Great Western Company. And further that the Great Western Railway Company might promote and construct a branch to Padstow. Now it is hereby mutually agreed by and between the Companies parties hereto as follows the Wadebridge Company being made parties hereto for the purpose of giving and so far as may be legally necessary to give effect to the engagement herein entered into by the South Western Company with regard to the Bodmin and Wadebridge Line and hereby undertaking to do whatever may be necessary to give effect to such arrangements accordingly.

1. The Great Western Company shall construct a junction between their Bodmin Branch and the Bodmin and Wadebridge Line at Boscarne Mill in accordance with and in manner shown upon the plans relating thereto to be agreed between and signed by William Jacomb the engineer in chief of the South Western Company and Lancaster Owen the engineer of the Great Western Company and the South Western Company shall afford all necessary facilities for such construction subject to the terms and conditions hereinafter appearing.

2. In the construction of such junction all openings of the Rails of the Bodmin and Wadebridge Railway and all interference with such Railway shall be made in accordance with and in manner shown upon the said Plans and all communications and openings and all necessary works and signalling arrangements at or near such junction shall be made by and so far as the same are coloured blue upon such Plans at the expense of the Great Western Company and such last mentioned works shall be for ever thereafter maintained in good repair by the South Western Company at the expense of the Great Western Company and so as not in any wise unduly to injure or prejudice the Railway or works of the Bodmin and Wadebridge Railway or unduly to interfere with or interrupt the traffic thereon. Provided always that by the construction of such junction the Great Western Company shall acquire only an easement or right of using the land necessary for the purpose of effecting such junction but no other interest therein. Such junction shall for all purposes be deemed to be a junction between the Bodmin Branch Railway of the Great Western Company authorised by the Great Western Railway (No. 1) Act 1882 and the Bodmin and Wadebridge Railway and all the provisions with regard to junctions in the Railways Clauses Act 1863 contained shall apply to such junction accordingly.

3. The South Western Company shall forthwith in accordance with plans to be agreed and signed as aforesaid purchase such land as may be necessary for the improvement of the curve near Grogley Bridge on the Bodmin and Wadebridge Line between Boscarne Mill Junction and Wadebridge and for the construction of a passenger station and goods shed and sidings in connection therewith to the eastward of the High Road at Wadebridge according to plans to be agreed and signed as aforesaid.

4. The South Western Company shall thereupon with all reasonable despatch proceed to the extent and in manner shown upon the plans agreed and signed as aforesaid to improve the aforesaid curve upon the Bodmin and Wadebridge Line and relay so far as may be necessary the portion thereof between the junction provided by Article 1 and Wadebridge and so as to adapt such Line for the passage of passenger and goods trains as a single Line of Rail and of the gauge of 4 feet 8½ inches to the satisfaction in all respects of the Board of Trade.

5. The South Western Company shall in accordance with the plans agreed and signed as aforesaid forthwith construct the said passenger station and goods shed and sidings in connection therewith.

6. The South Western Company will maintain the said portion of Railway station goods shed sidings and works in a proper and sufficient state for the passage of the traffic to be accommodated thereon.

7. Upon the said curve being improved the line relaid and the station goods shed and sidings constructed at Wadebridge as aforesaid the Great Western Company shall be at liberty to run over and use with their servants and with their engines carriages and wagons for all descriptions of traffic the portion of the Bodmin and Wadebridge Line between the said junction at Boscarne and Wadebridge.

8. The Great Western Company shall be entitled to have their own cartage agents booking and invoicing clerks and an inspector at Wadebridge Station together with the necessary accommodation for their staff thereat.

9. Except as provided by Article 8 the South Western Company shall provide the staff at the Wadebridge passenger station requisite for dealing with the Great Western passenger traffic and the Great Western Company shall pay the cost incurred in providing such staff and in case any difference shall arise as to the staff requisite for dealing with the Great Western traffic such difference shall be settled by Arbitration.

10. The South Western Company shall provide the requisite staff at and shall be entitled for the services of such staff and for the use of the Goods Shed and Sidings to the terminals at Wadebridge (less a reasonable allowance thereout to the Great Western Company for cartage of traffic carried at collected and delivered rates and any other expenses which they may incur at the Wadebridge Station) such terminals in respect of general merchandise and mineral traffic (except iron ore sand lime coal and coke) to be in accordance with Railway Clearing House regulations and in respect of iron ore sand lime coal and coke the terminals to be the sum of 3d. per ton. Provided always that should circumstances arise rendering it necessary for a lower terminal to be fixed for china clay and stone or any other material of a special or mineral class such commuted terminal shall be agreed or failing agreement settled by arbitration.

11. The South Western Company shall be entitled to receive in respect of all traffic carried by the Great Western Company over the Bodmin and Wadebridge Line by way of toll a mileage proportion after the deduction of Terminals of the receipts from all traffic less a reasonable allowance to the Great Western Company for working expenses having regard to the provisions under which the traffic is worked. Such allowance for a period of five years from the date when the running powers hereunder shall first be exercised to be at the rate of 27½ per cent.

12. If the amount payable by the Great Western Company to the South Western Company by way of toll under this Agreement shall not amount in any one year as a minimum to a sum equal to 8 per cent. upon the amount of the outlay incurred by the South Western Company in improving curves and relaying and adapting the line as aforesaid the Great Western Company will pay to the South Western Company the difference between the actual amount of such toll

payable and accruing to the South Western Company under this Agreement and interest at the rate of 8 per cent. upon such outlay which shall cover and include the cost of the maintenance of the works in respect of which such outlay has been incurred and the portion of the Line over which such running powers are exercised. Provided that the Great Western Company shall be at liberty to require the revision of this Article at the expiration of the first 5 years of this Agreement or at any time thereafter and regard shall also be had to the then user of the Line by any Company other than the Great Western.

13. The Great Western Company shall be at liberty to fix their own rates and fares for traffic carried by them over the Bodmin and Wadebridge Line to and from purely non-competitive Stations on the Great Western system the rates and fares for traffic to and from competitive stations to be agreed between the Companies or in case of difference settled by arbitration. In the event of the South Western Company objecting to any rates or fares fixed by the Great Western Company the South Western Company shall be entitled to require that the proportion accruing to the South Western Company shall be reviewed and in case of difference settled by arbitration.

14. Until any other Company than the Great Western Company use the Wadebridge Passenger Station the Great Western Company shall pay to the South Western Company by way of rent for the user of such Station a sum equal to 8 per cent. on the cost incurred in constructing such Station including any additional land that may be necessarily purchased for such Station such rent to cover also the cost of maintenance.

15. In arriving at the cost incurred in respect of the works mentioned in Articles 4 5 and 14 interest during construction shall be added at the rate of 4 per cent. per annum on the payments made from the time when the same shall be respectively so made.

16. Until any other Company than the Great Western Company use the Wadebridge passenger station the Great Western Company shall pay to the South Western Company half-yearly any additional cost incurred by them in respect of rates and taxes inclusive of gas and water in connection with such station.

17. The accounts of all moneys due by one Company to the other under this Agreement shall be settled monthly and the amount found due from one to the other shall be paid over to the Company entitled thereto at the expiration of every six months that is to say within 40 days after the 1st day of January and the 1st day of July in every year during the continuance of this agreement.

18. In case an interval less than an half year shall elapse between the first exercise by the Great Western Company of running powers under this Agreement and the 30th day of June or 31st day of December as the case may be next following the provisions of the preceeding article shall apply *mutatis mutandis* to such shorter period.

19. This Agreement shall take effect from the completion of the works to be constructed by the South Western Company under this Agreement and the approval thereof by the Inspecting Officer of the Board of Trade and shall continue in perpetuity.

20. Any difference which shall arise between the two Companies touching the true intent or construction or the effect incidents or consequences of these presents or touching the manner in which any of the provisions of these presents shall be carried into effect or touching the performance or observance of these presents or touching any breach or alleged breach of any of the Articles of these presents or any claim in connection therewith or otherwise relating to these premises shall be referred to such person as may be agreed upon between the Companies or as failing agreement shall be nominated on the application of either party by the Chairman for the time being of the North Eastern Railway Company and his decision shall

be final and binding on the two Companies as if the matter had been referred to arbitration and determined in accordance with the provisions of "The Railway Companies Arbitration Act 1859."

IN WITNESS WHEREOF the Companies parties hereto have caused their respective Common Seals to be hereunto affixed the day and year first above written.

The Common Seal of the London and South
Western Railway Company was hereunto
affixed in the presence of
FRED J. MACAULAY, *Secretary.*

The
Common Seal
of the
London and South
Western Railway
Company.

The Common Seal of the Bodmin and Wadebridge
Railway Company was hereunto
affixed in the presence of
FRED J. MACAULAY, *Secretary.*

The
Common Seal
of the
Bodmin and Wade-
bridge Railway
Company.

The Common Seal of the Great Western
Railway Company was hereunto
affixed in the presence of
J. D. HIGGINS, *Secretary.*

The
Common Seal
of the
Great Western
Railway
Company.

APPENDIX THREE

PRINCIPAL DIMENSIONS OF B&W ENGINES

	Camel	*Elephant*
Driving wheels (diam.)	3' 10"	3' 10"
Cylinders	10½" x 24"	12½" x 24"
Boiler pressure	50 lbs psi	50 lbs psi
Tubes	38 (4' 6" x 3")	65 (2' 2" x 3")
Firebox	4' 6" x 3' 6" x 1' 4"	4' 2" x 3' 6" x 1' 4"
Chimney	7' 10" x 12½"	9' 4" x 1' 3"
Net weight	5 tons 5 cwt	6 tons 10 cwt
Weight in working order	12 tons 5 cwt	14 tons 10 cwt
Tender laden weight	5 tons 10 cwt	
Tender capacity: water	370 gallons	
Tender capacity: coal	1 ton	
Net weight, engine and tender	10 tons 5 cwt	12 tons 5 cwt

PRINCIPAL DIMENSIONS OF PRESERVED B&W CARRIAGES

	Length	Width	Height	Wheelbase	Weight ton	cwt	qtr	Number of comts	seats
Composite	14'	6' 6½"	8' 5"	7' 6"	3	5	0	3	24
2nd class	10'	6' 5"	8' 5"	6' 4"	2	5	2	2	16
3rd class open	14' 10"	6' 5½"	5' 10½"	6' 9"	2	18	1	3	24
3rd class open	10'	6' 4½"	5' 5"	4' 6"	1	19	0	2	16

BODMIN AND WADEBRIDGE RAILWAY.

PASSENGER TRAINS,

October, 1871,

AND UNTIL FURTHER NOTICE.

MONDAY:	Wadebridge to Bodmin,	at	10. 0	A.M.
	Bodmin, to Wadebridge,	„	4. 0	P.M.
WEDNESDAY:	Wadebridge to Bodmin,	„	10. 0	A.M.
	Bodmin to Wadebridge,	„	4. 0	P.M.
FRIDAY:	Wadebridge to Bodmin,	„	10. 0	A.M.
	Bodmin to Wadebridge,	„	1. 0	P.M.
SATURDAY:	Wadebridge to Bodmin,	„	1. 0	P.M.
	Bodmin to Wadebridge,	„	2.30	„
	Wadebridge to Bodmin,	„	4.30	„
	Bodmin to Wadebridge,	„	7. 0	„

H. KYD, Superintendent.

LIDDELL and SON, Printers, BODMIN.

BODMIN AND WADEBRIDGE RAILWAY.

ROYAL CORNWALL
AGRICULTURAL EXHIBITION,
BODMIN.

WEDNESDAY & THURSDAY,

12th and 13th JUNE, 1872.

TRAINS will run as follows:

Wadebridge to Bodmin.	Bodmin to Wadebridge.
8 o'clock, Morning.	9 o'clock, Morning.
11 ,, ,,	12.30 ,, Noon.
2 ,, Afternoon.	9 ,, Evening.
7 ,, Evening.	

QUINTRELL, PRINTER AND BOOKBINDER, WADEBRIDGE.

Bodmin and Wadebridge Railway.

SWIMMING
MATCH,
BLACKPOOL,
WEDNESDAY, August 7, 1872.

TRAINS WILL RUN AS FOLLOW :

WADEBRIDGE TO BODMIN, - - - - - - -	10 A. M.
BODMIN TO BLACKPOOL, - - - - - - -	12.30 Noon.
BLACKPOOL TO BODMIN, - - - - - - -	6.30 P. M.
DUNMEER TO WADEBRIDGE, - - - - - - -	7 ,,

FARES :

WADEBRIDGE to DUNMEER and back,	9d.
BODMIN TO BLACKPOOL and back,	6d.

APPENDIX FOUR – TIMETABLES

1st June to 30th September 1909 or until further notice.

DOWN LONDON & SOUTH WESTERN AND UP GREAT WESTERN TRAINS – WEEKDAYS ONLY

Station		1 SW Car	2 SW Car	3 GW Pass	4 SW Mixed	5 SW Car	6 GW Pass	7 SW Min.Q.	8 SW Car	9 GW Pass	10 SW Min.Q.	11 SW Car	12 SW Car
WADEBRIDGE	dep	6.15	7.05	7.48	8.43	9.34	9.48	9.58	10.27	11.38	11.48	12.16	1.05
Grogley Halt		6.22	7.12			9.41			10.34			12.23	1.12
Nanstallon Halt		6.26½	7.16½			9.45½			10.38½			12.27½	1.16½
Boscarne Junction	arr	6.27½	7.17½	7.57	8.54	9.46½	9.57		10.39½	11.47		12.28½	1.17½
Boscarne Junction	dep	6.28	7.18	7.58	8.55	9.47	9.58	10.11	10.40	11.48	12.15	12.29	1.18
BODMIN GW	arr			8.08			10.08			11.58			
Dunmere Halt		6.30	7.20			9.49			10.42			12.31	1.20
BODMIN L&SW	arr	6.34	7.24		9.00	9.53			10.46			12.35	1.24

Station		13 GW Mixed	14 SW Goods E	15 SW Goods SX	16 SW Mixed SO	17 GW Goods E	18 GW Goods Q	19 GW Pass	20 SW Car	21 SW Car	22 SW Car	23 GW Mixed	24 GW Pass
WADEBRIDGE	dep	1.45	1.57	2.37	2.37	2.48		3.43	4.10	4.54	6.02	6.17	8.21
Grogley Halt									4.17	5.01	6.09		
Nanstallon Halt									4.21½	5.05½	6.13½		
Boscarne Junction	arr	1.55	2.09	2.49	2.48	3.00	3.29	3.52	4.22½	5.06½	6.14½	6.27	
Boscarne Junction	dep	1.56		2.53	2.49	3.07	3.39	3.53	4.23	5.07	6.15	6.28	
BODMIN GW	arr	2.08						4.03				6.40	
Dunmere Halt									4.25	5.09	6.17		
BODMIN L&SW	arr			2.59	2.54				4.29	5.13	6.21		

Station		25 SW Car	26 GW Pass B SO
WADEBRIDGE	dep	8.32	10.20
Grogley Halt		8.39	
Nanstallon Halt		8.43½	
Boscarne Junction	arr	8.44½	10.29
Boscarne Junction	dep	8.45	10.30
BODMIN GW	arr		10.40
Dunmere Halt		8.47	
BODMIN L&SW	arr	8.51	

1st June to 30th September 1909 or until further notice.
UP LONDON & SOUTH WESTERN AND DOWN GREAT WESTERN TRAINS – WEEKDAYS ONLY

		1 SW Car	2 GW Pass	3 SW Car	4 SW Pass	5 GW Pass	6 SW Car	7 SW Car	8 GW Pass	9 SW Car	11 GW Mixed	12 GW Goods E	13 SW Car
BODMIN L&SW	dep	6.43		8.19	9.08		10.07	10.50		12.40			2.19
Dunmere Halt		6.47		8.23	C		10.11	10.54		12.44			2.23
BODMIN GW	dep	6.48	7.12	8.24	9.11	9.17	10.12	10.55	11.13	12.45	1.12	1.42	2.24
Boscarne Junction	arr	6.48½	7.19	8.24½	9.12	9.22	10.12½	10.55½	11.18	12.45½	1.19	1.47	2.24½
Boscarne Junction	dep	6.50	7.20½	8.26		9.23	10.14	10.57	11.19	12.47	1.20	2.00	2.26
Nanstallon Halt					C								
Grogley Halt		6.53½		8.29½	C		10.17½	11.00½		12.50½			2.29½
WADEBRIDGE	arr	7.00	7.31	8.36	9.21	9.32	10.24	11.07	11.29	12.57	1.31	2.12	2.36

		14 SW Goods E	15 GW Pass	16 GW Goods Q	17 SW Mineral Q	18 SW Goods	19 SW Goods Q	20 SW Car B	21 GW Pass B	22 SW Car	23 SW Car	24 GW Pass	25 SW Car
BODMIN L&SW	dep					3.50		4.33		5.35	7.44		9.10
Dunmere Halt								4.37		5.39	7.48		9.14
BODMIN GW	dep		3.08	3.15				4.38	5.17	5.40	7.49	7.56	9.15
Boscarne Junction	arr		3.13	3.21		3.55		4.38½	5.22	5.40½	7.49½	8.01	9.15½
Boscarne Junction	dep	3.00	3.14		3.25	3.57	4.27	4.40	5.23	5.42	7.51	8.02	9.17
Nanstallon Halt													
Grogley Halt								4.43½		5.45½	7.54½		9.20½
WADEBRIDGE	arr	3.12	3.24		3.42	4.09	4.37	4.50	5.33	5.52	8.01	8.12	9.27

		26 GW Pass SO F
BODMIN L&SW	dep	
Dunmere Halt		
BODMIN GW	dep	9.57
Boscarne Junction	arr	10.02
Boscarne Junction	dep	10.03
Nanstallon Halt		
Grogley Halt		
WADEBRIDGE	arr	10.13

B Runs 4 minutes later during July, August and September.
C Calls at Dunmere, Nanstallon and Grogley on the second Tuesday in each month.
E Nos. 14 Down and 14 Up will run when required and as ordered by Wadebridge. They will not run when No. 17 Down and 12 Up run.
F July, August and September only.
Q Runs when required.
SO Saturdays only.
SX Saturdays excepted.

17th July 1932 and until further notice.

WEEKDAYS

		SR Car V	SR Mixed M	GW Pass	SR Car	SR Mineral BQ	SR Mineral BQ	GW Pass K	GW Pass P	SR Mixed A
WADEBRIDGE	dep	7.05	8.25	9.42	9.56	10.11	10.11	11.50	12.00	12.55
Grogley Halt		7.13	8.34		10.04					1.04
Nanstallon Halt		7.17½	8.39		10.08½					1.09½
Boscarne Junction	arr					10.34	10.55			
Boscarne Junction	dep	7.19	8.40½	9.54	10.10	10.50	11.09	12.02	12.12	1.11
BODMIN GW	arr			10.02				12.10	12.20	
Dunmere Halt		7.21	8.43½		10.12					1.14
BODMIN SR	arr	7.25	8.48		10.16					1.19

		GW pass	GW Mineral	GW Freight Q	SR Mixed	GW Mixed	GW Cattle Q	SR Car M	GW Pass P	SR Car
WADEBRIDGE	dep	1.40			3.14	3.35	3.50	5.13	5.30	6.10
Grogley Halt					3.22			5.21		6.18
Nanstallon Halt					3.26½			5.25½		6.22½
Boscarne Junction	arr					3.48	4.03			
Boscarne Junction	dep	1.52	2.05	3.13	3.29	3.58	4.09	5.27	5.42	6.24
BODMIN GW	arr	2.00	2.19	3.27			4.17		5.50	
Dunmere Halt					3.32			5.29		6.26
BODMIN SR	arr				3.37			5.33		6.30

17th July 1932 and until further notice.

SUNDAY 28th AUGUST ONLY applies to the "SR Empty" and "SR Return Exc'h" columns.

Station		GW Pass	SR Car M	GW Pass L	SR Car E	GW Pass SO	SR Empty	SR Return Exc'h
WADEBRIDGE	dep	7.00	8.14	8.35	9.42	9.55	(am) 9†30	(pm) 10.55
Grogley Halt			8.22		9.50			11.03
Nanstallon Halt			8.26½		9.54½			11.08½
Boscarne Junction	arr							
Boscarne Junction	dep	7.12	8.28	8.47	9.56½	10.07	9.41	11.09
BODMIN GW	arr	7.20		8.55		10.15		
Dunmere Halt	arr		8.30		9.58		9†46	11.11
BODMIN SR	arr		8.34		10.02			11.15

WEEKDAYS

Station		SR Car G	SR Mineral Q	GW Pass	GW Mixed	SR Car K	GW Pass	GW Mineral D	SR Mixed A	SR Freight Q	GW Engine & Van Q
BODMIN SR	dep	7.32	8.56			11.28			2.05		
Dunmere Halt		7.36	9.00			11.32			2.10		
BODMIN GW	dep			9.10	10.53		1.09	1.30		2.30	2.38
Boscarne Junction	arr	7.37½	9.01½	9.16	11.00	11.33½	1.15	1.37	2.12	2.37	2.44
Boscarne Junction	dep	7.39	9.03			11.35			2.14		2.48
Nanstallon Halt		7.43½	9.07½			11.39½			2.19		
Grogley Halt											
WADEBRIDGE	arr	7.51	9.15	9.27	11.12	11.47	1.26		2.28		3.00

WEEKDAYS

Station		GW Pass	SR Mineral Q	SR Car F	GW Pass P	GW Pass K	SR Car	GW Pass D	GW Pass X	SR Car G	GW Pass
BODMIN SR	dep		3.45	4.23			5.39			6.37	
Dunmere Halt				4.27			5.43			6.41	
BODMIN GW	dep	2.56			4.43	4.55		6.19	6.25		7.55
Boscarne Junction	arr	3.02		4.28½	4.49	5.01	5.44½	6.25	6.31	6.42½	8.01
Boscarne Junction	dep		4.15	4.30			5.46			6.44	
Nanstallon Halt				4.34½			5.50½			6.48½	
Grogley Halt											
WADEBRIDGE	arr	3.13	4.28	4.42	5.00	5.12	5.56	6.36	6.42	6.56	8.12

17th July 1932 and until further notice.

		SR Car G	GW Pass. SO	SR Car E	SUNDAY 28th AUGUST ONLY	
---	---	---	---	---	SR Half Day Exc'n to Paignton (am)	SR Empty (pm)
BODMIN SR	dep	8.45		10.10	10.00	11†25
Dunmere Halt		8.49		10.14	10.04	
BODMIN GW	dep		9.30			
Boscarne Junction	arr					
Boscarne Junction	dep	8.50½	9.36	10.15½	10.05½	11.30
Nanstallon Halt		8.52½		10.17	10.07	
Grogley Halt		8.58½		10.23½	10.11½	
WADEBRIDGE	arr	9.06	9.47	10.31	10.19	11†42

A   Will not convey wagons to or from Boscarne Junction. Bodmin SR freight traffic to or from the GW line to be sent via Wadebridge

B   Alternate timings

D   Not Saturdays 18th July to 9th September; daily commencing 12th September

E   Wednesdays to 7th September only

F   Runs to Padstow commencing 12th September. Train men to be prepared to stop as and when signalled by ganger for the purpose of taking up permanent way staff only

G   To Padstow

K   Until 10th September

L   Not to convey cattle, etc traffic

M   From Padstow

P   From 12th September

V   Stops as and when required to set down permanent way staff only

X   Saturdays only, 23rd July to 10th September

SO   Saturdays only

SX   Saturdays excepted

Q   Runs when required

SR   Up and Down Passenger Trains and Cars call when required at the Shooting Range Platform (situated about 1½ miles from Wadebridge) to set down or take up Territorials proceeding from or to Bodmin or Wadebridge. Bodmin and Wadebridge to arrange.

(Note the use of the description "Car" to denote a SR passenger train)

70

18th June 1962 and until further notice.

WEEKDAYS ONLY

Group 1

		Z*			*	SX Freight	M	Z
From Padstow				8.12	9.03 (X)			
WADEBRIDGE	dep	6.55	7.58	8.30	9.18	9.35	9.48	9.50
Grogley Halt		7.03	8.06	8.38			9.56	9.58
Nanstallon Halt		7.07½	8.10½	8.42½	9.30½		10.00½	10.02½
Boscarne Junction	arr	7/09	8/12	8/44	9/32	9.48	10/02	10/04
Boscarne Junction	dep	7.17		8.53	9.40	10.21		
BODMIN GENERAL	arr	K		K	K	To Wenford		
Dunmere Halt			8.14				10.04	10.06
BODMIN NORTH	arr		8.18				10.08	10.10

Group 2

		Z*	M*	Freight	Z	M SDO*	M Freight	Z*
From Padstow		10.57	11.35	11.55 (X)	12.10			
WADEBRIDGE	dep	11.09	11.54	12.15	12.25	12.28	1.02	1.25
Grogley Halt					12.33	12.36		1.33
Nanstallon Halt		11.21½	12.06½		12.37½	12.40½	1.17	1.37½
Boscarne Junction	arr	11/23	12/08	12.29	12/39	12/42	1.29	1/39
Boscarne Junction	dep	11.31	12.15		12.41		1.37	1.47
BODMIN GENERAL	arr	K	K		12.45			K
Dunmere Halt						12.44		
BODMIN NORTH	arr					12.48		

Group 3

		M*	M Freight	Z* Freight	Z	*	M	Z
From Padstow				2.52			4.40	
WADEBRIDGE	dep	1.28	1.43	3.09	3.24	4.43	5.11	5.12
Grogley Halt		1.36		3.17		4.54	5.19	5.20
Nanstallon Halt		1.40½	1.58	3.21½		4.55½	5.23½	5.24½
Boscarne Junction	arr	1/42	2.08	3/23	3/36	5.00	5/25	5/26
Boscarne Junction	dep	1.50		3.25	3.44	5.08		
BODMIN GENERAL	arr	K			K			
Dunmere Halt				3.25			5.27	5.28
BODMIN NORTH	arr		2.16	3.29			5.31	5.32

Group 4

		W*	E*	M*	*	H	H
From Padstow		5.02 (V)	5.24	5.24		7.35	7.35
WADEBRIDGE	dep	5.27	5.34	6.12	7.00	7.55	8.55
Grogley Halt				6.20		8.03	
Nanstallon Halt		5.39½	5.46½	6.24½	7.12½	8.07½	9.07½
Boscarne Junction	arr	5/41	5/48	6/26	7/14	8/09	9/09
Boscarne Junction	dep	5.49	5.56	6.33	7.21	8.17	9.17
BODMIN GENERAL	arr	K	K	K	K	K	K
Dunmere Halt							
BODMIN NORTH	arr						

18th July 1962 and until further notice.

WEEKDAYS ONLY

			*		Z	M	Z*	M*
			7.50 from Bod. Rd				10.05 from Bod. Rd	10.10 from Bod. Rd
BODMIN NORTH	dep			8.43				
Dunmere Halt				8.47				
BODMIN GENERAL	dep	7.27	8.08	8/48½ / 8.50	8.58	8†59	10.20	10.35
Boscarne Junction	arr	7/33	8/14	8.54½	9/05	9/05	10/26	10/41
Boscarne Junction	dep	7.34½	8.15½					
Nanstallon Halt		7.39						
Grogley Halt								
WADEBRIDGE	arr	P7.47½	P8.27	9.02	9.16	9†16	P10.37	P10.52

		*	Z* Freight	M*	Z	M	Z* Freight	M Freight	Z*
				12.20 from Bod. Rd	12.43 from Bod. Rd				2.30 from Bod. Rd
BODMIN NORTH	dep	11.20				2.00			
Dunmere Halt		11.24				2.04			
BODMIN GENERAL	dep	11/25½ / 11.27	11.40	12.38	12.56	2/05½ / 2.07	2.15	2.27	2.48
Boscarne Junction	arr	11.31½	11.53	12/44	1/02	2.11½	2.23	2.35	2/54
Boscarne Junction	dep			12.45½	1.03½		2.28	2.40	
Nanstallon Halt									
Grogley Halt									
WADEBRIDGE	arr	X11.39		12.57	1.15	P2.19	2.43	2.55	3.05

		SDO *	SX Freight	M	Z	Z*	M*
			From Wenford 3.09		8.00 from Bod. Rd	4C25 from Bod. Rd	5.00 from Bod. Rd
BODMIN NORTH	dep			4.05	4.23		
Dunmere Halt				4.09	4.27		
BODMIN GENERAL	dep	1.08		4/10½ / 4.12	4/28½ / 4.30	4.50	5.19
Boscarne Junction	arr	1/14	3.45	4.16½	4.31½	4/56	5/26
Boscarne Junction	dep	1.15½				4.57½	5.27½
Nanstallon Halt							
Grogley Halt							
WADEBRIDGE	arr		3.58	P4.24	V4.42	X5.09	5.39

		M	Z	*	Z	H
					8.00 from Bod. Rd	9.42 from Bod. Rd
BODMIN NORTH	dep	5.36	5.44			
Dunmere Halt		5.40	5.48			
BODMIN GENERAL	dep	5/41½ / 5.43	5/49½ / 5.51	6.35	8.20	9.55
Boscarne Junction	arr	5.47½	5.55½	6/41	8/27	10.02
Boscarne Junction	dep			6.42½	8.28½	10.03½
Nanstallon Halt				6.47	8.32½	10.07½
Grogley Halt						
WADEBRIDGE	arr	5.55	6.03	P6.54½	V8.40	P10.15

*   Worked by Western Region.
/   Denotes passing time.
   Empty coaching stock.
SDO   Schooldays only, not advertised.
C   Dep. 4.34 until 7th September.
E   Mondays to Fridays only, 18th June to 7th September.
H   Weekdays until 8th September
K   To Bodmin Road.
P   To Padstow.
V   To or from Padstow commencing 10th September.
W   Weekdays commencing 10th September
X   To or from Padstow until 8th September.

14th June 1965 to 16th April 1966

WEEKDAYS ONLY
(NOT Saturdays 19th June to 4th September)

Station	EBV	*	DRB MO (from St. Blazey)	DRB MX	DRB	Freight SO	DRB	NA SX	LE SX	*	DRB	Freight SO
PADSTOW *(dep)*								8.16		8.45		
WADEBRIDGE *(arr)*								8.25		8.54		
WADEBRIDGE *(dep)*		6.55		7+20		7.35		8X28		8.55		
Grogley Halt		7.02						8.35		9.02		
Nanstallon Halt		7.06						8.39		9.06		
Boscarne Junction *(arr)*						7.48				9.08		
Boscarne Junction *(dep)*			7+30	7/30	8+02	8.04		8/41		9.09	9.10	9.20
Dunmere Halt *(arr)*			7+35	7+35	8+08	8.12					9.11½	
BODMIN NORTH *(arr)*								8.48			9.15	
BODMIN GENERAL *(arr)*		7.15								9.15		9.35
BODMIN GENERAL *(dep)*	5.35	7.18							9‖00	9.18		10.00
BODMIN ROAD *(arr)*	5.45	7.25							9‖10	9.25		10.22

Station	Freight SX	Freight SX (to Wenford Bridge)	*	DRB	Freight	EBV SX Q	Freight SO (to St. Blazey)	*	DRB	Freight SX	Freight SX
PADSTOW *(dep)*			10.45					12.45			
WADEBRIDGE *(arr)*			10.54					12.54			
WADEBRIDGE *(dep)*	9.10		10.55		12.15			12.55			
Grogley Halt			11.02					1.02			
Nanstallon Halt			11.06					1.06			
Boscarne Junction *(arr)*	9.24		11.08					1.08			
Boscarne Junction *(dep)*	9.35	10.25	11.09	11.10	12/26			1.09	1.10		
Dunmere Halt *(arr)*				11.11½					1.11½		
BODMIN NORTH *(arr)*	9.43			11.15	12.36				1.15		
BODMIN GENERAL *(arr)*			11X15			12.45	12.45	1.15		2.40	2.50
BODMIN GENERAL *(dep)*			11.18			12.55	1.02	1.18		2.55	2.58
BODMIN ROAD *(arr)*			11.25					1.25		3.19	3.35

14th June 1965 to 16th April 1966

	*	DRB	DRB	DRB	DRB *	DRB *	From 27 Sept	FO Until 3 Sept	*	DRB	DRB Freight SX	* To Halwill	DRB SO	*
PADSTOW .... dep	2.37						5.00	5†00				5.30		6.55
WADEBRIDGE ...... arr	2.46						5.09	5†09				5.39		7.04
WADEBRIDGE ...... dep	2.47				4†10				5.20		5.35	5.40	6.35	7.05
Grogley Halt .... dep	2.54								5.27					7.12
Nanstallon Halt .... dep	2.58								5.31					7.16
Boscarne Junction .. arr	3.00				4/20				5.33		5/47			
Boscarne Junction .. dep	3.01	3.05	4†00		4†24	5†05			5.34	5.35			6/45	7/18
Dunmere Halt ...... arr		3.06½								5.36½				
BODMIN NORTH .. arr		3.10	4†06			5†15				5.40				
BODMIN GENERAL arr	3.07								5.40		6.00		6.51	7.24
BODMIN GENERAL dep	3.10			4.10					5.43		6X17		6.53	7X26
BODMIN ROAD ...... arr	3.17			4.17					5.50		6.33		7.00	7.33

SATURDAYS 19th June to 4th Sept

	SX Freight to St. Blazey	* Until 25 Sept	DRB From Bodmin Road	DRB From Bodmin Road	*	DRB	*	DRB	* To Halwill
PADSTOW .... dep		8.30			8.30				10.20
WADEBRIDGE ...... arr		8.39			8.39				10.29
WADEBRIDGE ...... dep			6.50		8.40	9.25		10.00	
Grogley Halt .... dep			6.57		8.47			10.07	
Nanstallon Halt .... dep			7.01		8.51			10.11	
Boscarne Junction .. arr					8.53			10.13	
Boscarne Junction .. dep	8.15		7/03	7†41	8X55	9/36		10.14	10.15
Dunmere Halt ...... arr					9.01½				10.16½
BODMIN NORTH .. arr				7†45	9.05				10.20
BODMIN GENERAL arr	8.30		7.10		9.00	9.42	9.45	10.20	
BODMIN GENERAL dep	8.54		7.13			9.48		10X23	
BODMIN ROAD ...... arr	9.10		7.20			9.55	9.55	10.30	

14th June 1965 to 16th April 1966

		DRB	DRB	*	DRB	*	DRB	*	DRB	DRB	* To Exeter Cen
PADSTOW	dep		11.20	12.15	1.15	2.05		4.05		5.02	5.30
WADEBRIDGE	arr		11.29	12.24	1.24	2.14		4.14		5.11	5.39
WADEBRIDGE	dep		11.30	12.25	1.25	2.15	2.54	4.15		5.12	5.40
Grogley Halt			11.37	12.32		2.22		4.22			
Nanstallon Halt			11.41	12.36		2.26		4.26			
Boscarne Junction	arr		11.43		1.35		3.04	4.28			
Boscarne Junction	dep	10†40	11.44	12/37½	1X36	2/28	3.05	4X30		5/22	
Dunmere Halt	arr		11.47 / 11.48½		1.40 / 1.40½		3.06 / 3.07½	4.30 / 4.31½	5+18		
BODMIN NORTH	arr	10†45	11.52		1.45		3.11	4.35	5+23		
BODMIN GENERAL	arr		11.50	12.34	1.42	2.34	3.11	4.36		5.28	
BODMIN GENERAL	dep		11.56	12.46	1.48	2.37	3X22	4.39		5.35	
BODMIN ROAD	arr		12.03	12.53	1.55	2.44	3.29	4.46		5.42	

		*	DRB To St. Blazey	*	LE To St. Blazey
PADSTOW	dep	6.20		7.10	9.00
WADEBRIDGE	arr	6.29		7.19	9.09
WADEBRIDGE	dep	6X35		7.20	9‖20
Grogley Halt		6.42		7.27	
Nanstallon Halt		6.46		7.31	
Boscarne Junction	arr	6.48		7/33	9/30
Boscarne Junction	dep	6.49	7†15		
Dunmere Halt	arr	6.50 / 6.51½			
BODMIN NORTH	arr	6.55			
BODMIN GENERAL	arr	6.55	7.20	7.39	9.35
BODMIN GENERAL	dep	6.58	7.25	7.46	9.40
BODMIN ROAD	arr	7.05	7†35	7.53	9‖50

14th June 1965 to 16th April 1966

WEEKDAYS ONLY
(NOT Saturdays 19th June to 4th Sept)

Station		Freight	Freight	DRB MO from St Blazey	MO Until 6 Sept	DRB	*	Freight SO	DRB	DRB	DRB	*	Freight SX
BODMIN ROAD	dep	5.00	6.00	6†52			7.45		8.32			9.50	
BODMIN GENERAL	arr	5.15	6.15	7.00			7.53		8.40			9.58	
BODMIN GENERAL	dep		6.25	7X20			7.55			8†55		10.00	
BODMIN NORTH	dep					7.50		8.30			9.55		10.05
Dunmere Halt						7.53½					9.58½		
Boscarne Junction	arr					7.55	8.00				10.00	10.05	
Boscarne Junction	dep		6/37	7†25			8.01	8.38		9†00		10.06	10.13
Nanstallon Halt							8.03					10.08	
Grogley Halt			6.48				8.07					10.12	
WADEBRIDGE	arr						8.14					10.19	
WADEBRIDGE	dep				7†55		8X31					10.21	
PADSTOW	arr				8†05		8.40					10.30	

Station		Freight	DRB	*	Freight K SX	Freight SX 1.35 Wenford Bridge	DRB	*	Freight SX	* From 27 Sept From Halwill	DRB	*	LE SX
BODMIN ROAD	dep	10.45		11.40	1.30			1.53				3.37	3II50
BODMIN GENERAL	arr	11.00		11.48	1.45			2.01				3.45	3II58
BODMIN GENERAL	dep	11X20		11.50	2.10			2.03				3.47	
BODMIN NORTH	dep		11.45				2.00		3.30		3.45		
Dunmere Halt			11.48½				2.03½				3.48½		
Boscarne Junction	arr		11.50	11.55			2.05	2.08			3.50	3.52	
Boscarne Junction	dep	11.42		11.56	2.25	2.35		2.09	3/38			3.53	
Nanstallon Halt				11.58				2.11				3.55	
Grogley Halt		11.55		12.02				2.15				3.59	
WADEBRIDGE	arr			12.09				2.22		3.54		4.06	
WADEBRIDGE	dep			12.11				2.23	3.50	4.09			
PADSTOW	arr			12.20				2.32		4.18			

14th June 1965 to 16th April 1966

Station		NA SX	*	DRB	*	DRB	*	* Freight SX	* Until 25 Sept
BODMIN ROAD	dep			4.30			6.05	7.00	7.45
BODMIN GENERAL	arr			4.38			6.13	7.15	7.53
BODMIN GENERAL	dep	4.15		4.42			6.15	7.30	7.55
BODMIN NORTH	dep		4.30			5.50			
Dunmere Halt			4.33½			5.53½		7.45	
Boscarne Junction	arr	4/21	4.35	4.47		5/55	6/20	8/00	
Boscarne Junction	dep	4.23	4.36	4.48		5.57	6.22	8.02	
Nanstallon Halt		4.27		4.50		6.01	6.26	8.06	
Grogley Halt				4.54			6.33		
WADEBRIDGE	arr	4.34	4.46	5.01		6.08	6.34	8.13	
WADEBRIDGE	dep	4.36			5.12				8.16
PADSTOW	arr	4.45			5.21		6.43		8.25

SATURDAYS
19th June to 4th Sept

Station		DRB To Bodmin North	DRB	*	* From Exeter Cen	DRB	*	DRB	DRB	DRB	*	*
BODMIN ROAD	dep	7†23		7.43			9.20		10.05		11.25	12.15
BODMIN GENERAL	arr	7.30		7.51			9.28		10.13		11.33	12.23
BODMIN GENERAL	dep	7.33		7.53			9.30		10.28		11.37	12.30
BODMIN NORTH	dep	7†38	7.50			9.25		10.25		11.32		
Dunmere Halt			7.53½			9.28½		10.28½		11.35½		
Boscarne Junction	arr		7.55	7.58		9.30	9.35	10.30	10.33	11.37	11.42	12.35
Boscarne Junction	dep			7.59			9X37		10.34		11X45	12X38
Nanstallon Halt				8.01			9.39		10.36		11.47	12.40
Grogley Halt				8.05			9.43		10.40		11.51	12.44
WADEBRIDGE	arr			8.12	8.46		9.50		10.47		11.58	12.51
WADEBRIDGE	dep			8.18	9.16				10.49		11.59	12.52
PADSTOW	arr			8.27	9.26				10.58		12.08	1.01

14th June 1965 to 16th April 1966

	DRB	*	DRB	DRB	DRB	*	* From Exeter Cen	DRB	*	DRB	DRB	DRB To St. Blazey
BODMIN ROAD .... dep		1.15		2.08		3.10	4.10		5.05		6.00	8.05
BODMIN GENERAL .... arr		1.23		2.16		3.18	4.18		5.13		6.08	8.13
BODMIN GENERAL .... dep		1.28		2.22		3.20	4.24		5.16		6.14	8.19
BODMIN NORTH .... dep	1.25		2.20		3.19			5.10		6.10		
Dunmere Halt .... dep	1.28½		2.23½		3.22½			5.13½		6.13½		7†05
Boscarne Junction ...... arr	1.30	1.33	2.25	2.27	3.24	3.25		5.15	5.21	6.15	6.19	7†10
Boscarne Junction ...... dep		1X36		2X29		3.26	4/29		5X23		6.20	8/24
Nanstallon Halt		1.38		2.31		3.28			5.25		6.22	8.26
Crogley Halt		1.42		2.35		3.32			5.29		6.26	8.30
WADEBRIDGE .... arr		1.49		2.42		3.39	4.39		5.36		6.33	8.37
WADEBRIDGE .... dep		1.50				3.41	4.40		5.38		6X36	8.38
PADSTOW .... arr		1.59				3.50	4.49		5.47		6.45	8.47

*	Diesel multiple unit
†	Empty coaching stock
=	Light engine
/	Denotes passing time
DRB	Diesel railbus
EBV	Engine and brake van
LE	Light engine
NA	Not advertised school train
FO	Fridays only
MO	Mondays only
MX	Mondays excepted
SO	Saturdays only
SX	Saturdays excepted
K	From Bodmin Road to Bodmin General, only runs if required
Q	Runs if required
X	Crosses other train on single line

WADEBRIDGE AND WENFORD

1st June to 30th September 1909 or until further notice.
A Mineral Train, as required, will run on Week-days, as under:

	1		2	
	arr	dep	arr	dep
WADEBRIDGE		9.58		11.48
Grogley Halt			11.54	11.56
Ruthern Bridge			12.00	12.04
Grogley Halt			12.08	12.10
Boscarne Junction	10.11	10.30	12.15	12.55
Dunmere Junction	10.35	11.04	1.00	1.15
Helland	11.24	11.29	1.33	1.38
Tresarrett	11.39	11.49	1.48	1.56
Clay Co's Sdg	11.55	12.05	2.02	2.12
WENFORD	12.10		2.17	

	1		2	
	arr	dep	arr	dep
WENFORD		1.45		2.50
Clay Co's Sdg	1.50	2.00	2.55	3.05
Tresarrett	2.06	2.16	3.11	3.16
Helland	2.25	2.28	3.25	3.28
Dunmere Junction	2.49	3.00	3.48	4.05
Boscarne Junction	3.05	3.25	4.09	4.27
Nanstallon	3.28	3.32		
WADEBRIDGE	3.42		4.37	

When No. 1 runs No. 2 will not run, and when No. 2 runs No. 1 will not run. Wadebridge to arrange.

17th July 1932 and until further notice

WEEKDAYS ONLY — Alternative timings

	1		2				arr	dep
	arr	dep	arr	dep	WENFORD			1.35
WADEBRIDGE		10.11		10.11	Clay Co's Siding		1.40	2.15
Grogley			A		Tresarrett		2.20	2.30
Ruthern Bridge			A		Parkin's Siding }			
Grogley			10.44	10.49	Roadstone Co's Siding }		2.34	2.45
Nanstallon	10.21	10.31			Helland		2.54	2.59
Boscarne Junc	10.34	10.50	10.55	11.09	Dunmere Siding		A	
Dunmere Junc	10.55	11.15	11.14	11.33	Dunmere Junction		3.20	3.41
Dunmere Siding	A		A		Boscarne Junction		3.45	4.15
Helland	11.44	11.49	11.54	11.59	WADEBRIDGE		4.28	
Roadstone Co's Siding }								
Parkin's Siding }	11.58	12.08	12.08	12.18				
Tresarrett	12.12	12.22	12.22	12.32				
Clay Co's Siding	12.27	12.47	12.37	12.57				
WENFORD	12.51		1.01					

A Call if required only

18th July 1962 and until further notice

		SX				SX
WADEBRIDGE	dep	9.35a	WENFORD	dep	1.25
Boscarne Junction	arr	9.48	China Clay Co. Siding	arr	1.30
	dep	10.21		dep	1.55
Dunmere Junction		10/25	Tresarrett Siding	arr	2.00
Dunmere Siding	arr	10.26		dep	2.05
	dep	10.46	Dunmere Siding	arr	2.40
Tresarrett Siding	arr	11.26		dep	2.43
	dep	11.36	Dunmere Junction	arr	2.44
China Clay Co. Siding	arr	11.41		dep	3.04
	dep	12.37	Boscarne Junction	arr	3.09
WENFORD	arr	12.41		dep	3.45
			WADEBRIDGE	arr	3.58

a   On Thursdays stop at Speed Restriction Board at 2¼ mile post and on Fridays at Nanstallon Down Distant Signal to change lamps and run six minutes later to Boscarne Junction.

SX   Saturdays excepted

APPENDIX FIVE – ENGINE DIAGRAMS

Extracts of Engine Workings for passenger and freight trains
Southern Railway (Western Division) 26th September 1938 and until further notice.

WADEBRIDGE DUTY 604
0298 CLASS
Wadebridge Shunting Engine

also works

	Wadebridge	9.50 a.m.	**Mxd**
10. 4 a.m.	Padstow	11.35 a.m.	**F**
11.49 a.m.	Wadebridge		

WADEBRIDGE DUTY 606
02 CLASS

	Wadebridge Shed	6.40 a.m.	//
//	Wadebridge	7.00 a.m.	P
7.20 a.m.	Bodmin	7.27 a.m.	P
7.57 a.m.	Padstow	8.02 a.m.	P
8.11 a.m.	Wadebridge	8.19 a.m.	P
8.39 a.m.	Bodmin	9.00 a.m.	P
9.19 a.m.	Wadebridge	9.40 a.m.	P
10.00 a.m.	Bodmin	11.28 am.	P
11.47 a.m.	Wadebridge		

Engine Requirements

	Wadebridge	12.55 p.m.	**Mxd**
1.19 p.m.	Bodmin	2. 5 p.m.	**Mxd**
2.40 p.m.	Padstow	2.55 p.m.	**Mxd**
		ANR	
3. 4 p.m.	Wadebridge	3.14 p.m.	P
3.37 p.m.	Bodmin	4.23 p.m.	P
4.43 p.m.	Padstow	4.58 p.m.	P
5.30 p.m.	Bodmin	5.36 p.m.	P
5.55 p.m.	Wadebridge	6.10 p.m.	P
6.30 p.m.	Bodmin	6.37 p.m.	P
7.14 p.m.	Padstow	8. 2 p.m.	P
8.33 p.m.	Bodmin	8.45 p.m.	P
9.20 p.m.	Padstow	9.40 p.m.	P

Wednesdays Excepted

9.42 p.m.	Wadebridge	* *	//
* *	Wadebridge Shed		

Wednesdays Only

10. 2 p.m.	Bodmin	10.10 p.m.	P
10.31 p.m.	Wadebridge	* *	//
//	Wadebridge Shed		

WADEBRIDGE DUTY 607
0298 CLASS

	Wadebridge Shed	* *	//
//	Wadebridge	10.00 a.m.	F
12.51 p.m.	Wenford	1.35 p.m.	F
4.26 p.m.	Wadebridge Shed	* *	//
//	Wadebridge Shed		

OR

	Wadebridge Shed	* *	//
//	Wadebridge	7.35 a.m.	F
9.15 a.m.	Wenford C.C. Sdg	10. 0 a.m.	F
11. 9 a.m.	Boscarne Junction	11.40 a.m.	F
1.21 p.m.	Wenford	1.45 p.m.	F
4.26 p.m.	Wadebridge	* *	//
* *	Wadebridge Shed		

Explanatory notes

//	Light engine
ANR	Assisting, not required
F	Freight
Mxd	Mixed train
P	Passenger

Plymouth Division (former Southern Region lines)
issued by Line Manager's Office, Wimbledon for Divisional Manager, Plymouth

Weekdays 9th September 1963 and until further notice

LAIRA DUTY NO. 66 (A)
1100 H.P. D.6300 Class

As shown W.R. diagrams until AFTER

—	Liskeard	6.00 a.m.	/ /
6.15 a.m.	Bodmin Road	6.55 a.m.	
			Mxd
7. 5 a.m.	Bodmin General	7.20 a.m.	P
7.27 a.m.	Bodmin Road	7.50 a.m.	P
8.50 a.m.	Padstow	9. 3 a.m.	P
9.52 a.m.	Bodmin Road	10. 5 a.m.	P
10.49 a.m.	Padstow	10.57 a.m.	P
11.47 a.m.	Bodmin Road	12.20 p.m.	P
12.57 p.m.	Wadebridge	1.25 p.m.	P
2. 2 p.m.	Bodmin Road	2.30 p.m.	P
3. 5 p.m.	Wadebridge	3.24 p.m.	P
4. 1 p.m.	Bodmin Road	4.25 p.m.	P
5. 9 p.m.	Wadebridge	5.27 p.m.	P
6. 8 p.m.	Bodmin Road	6.17 p.m.	P
7. 9 p.m.	Padstow	7.35 p.m.	P
8.17 p.m.	Bodmin General	9. 0 p.m.	P
9. 7 p.m.	Bodmin Road	10. 5 p.m.	P
10.13 p.m.	Bodmin General	10.18 p.m.	/ /
10.23 p.m.	Bodmin Loco	—	

St. Blazey and Bodmin Men.

LAIRA DUTY No. 66 (B)
1100 H.P. D.6300 Class

As shown W.R. diagrams

—	Bodmin General	11.45 a.m.	F
11.58 a.m.	Boscarne Jc.	12.25 p.m.	F
12.34 p.m.	Bodmin General	12.50 p.m.	P
12.57 p.m.	Bodmin Road	1.32 p.m.	P
1.40 p.m.	Bodmin General	2. 5 p.m.	F
2.25 p.m.	Bodmin Road	3.20 p.m.	F
3.35 p.m.	Bodmin General (S.X.)	4. 8 p.m.	P
4.27 p.m.	Wadebridge (S.X.)	4.43 p.m.	P
5. 8 p.m.	Bodmin General	5.40 p.m.	P
5.47 p.m.	Bodmin Road	6.15 p.m.	/ /
6.43 p.m.	St. Blazey Loco	—	

St. Blazey and Bodmin Men.

EXMOUTH JC. DUTY No. 588.
5 F. (N. Class)

M.O. – Off No. 588 **Saturday.**
M.X. – Off No. 587, **S. X.**

–	Wadebridge Loco	12.50 p.m.	/ /
* *	Wadebridge	1. 2 p.m.	F
1.37 p.m.	Bodmin North	—	

F – Shunting 1.45 p.m. to 2.15 p.m.

—	Bodmin North	2.15 p.m.	F
2.43 p.m.	Wadebridge	* * / /	

SATURDAYS EXCEPTED.

* *	Loco Yard	4.25 p.m.	/ /
4.30 p.m.	Wadebridge	4.40 p.m.	F
12. 8 a.m.	Exmouth Jc	12.20 a.m.	/ /
12.23 a.m.	Exmouth Jc. Loco	—	

SATURDAYS ONLY

* *	Wadebridge Loco	—	
	Stable No. 588 **Mon.**		

Wadebridge Men.

(1) Off No 598 prepare work, 12.50 p.m. / /, etc. **(S.X.)**, relieved 4.40 p.m., then finish disposal of No 647, **(S.O.)** dispose.

(2) 1st set **(S.X.)** on duty 4.25 p.m., relieve 4.40 p.m., work to Launceston, change with No. 597 at 6.46 p.m., work, dispose and as ordered.

EXMOUTH JC. DUTY No. 591
4 P./5F (N. Class)

Off No. 590

—	Wadebridge Loco	7.30 a.m.	/ /
7.40 a.m.	Wadebridge	7.58 a.m.	P
8.18 a.m.	Bodmin North	8.43 a.m.	P
9. 2 am.	Wadebridge	9.10 a.m.	/ /
9.15 a.m.	Loco. Yard	11.15 a.m.	/ /
* *	Wadebridge	11.35 a.m.	F

SATURDAYS EXCEPTED

7.42 p.m.	Okehampton	—	

C– Shunting 8.30 p.m. to 9.00 p.m.

—	Okehampton	9.25 p.m.	
			Stone
10.43 p.m.	Exeter	10.49 p.m.	/ /
10.52 p.m.	Exmouth Jc	—	

Work No. 589.

SATURDAYS ONLY

7.30 p.m.	Okehampton	—	

C– Shunting 8.30 p.m. to 9.00 p.m.

—	Okehampton	9.30 p.m.	/ /
10.43 p.m.	Exmouth Jc. Loco	—	

Wadebridge Men.

(1) 1st set duty 6.30 a.m., work and relieved 11.25 a.m., relieve No. 646 at 11.47 a.m. and relieved 2.30 pm.

(2) 2nd set on duty 11.10 a.m. relieve 11.25 a.m. **(S.X)** work change to No. 587 at Launceston 2.30 p.m. work relieved Wadebridge 6.55 p.m. **(S.O.)** work, change to No. 597 at Halwill Jc. 6.21 p.m. work relieved Wadebridge 7.47 p.m.

WADEBRIDGE DUTY No. 645.
1 F.T. (13 XX Class)

—	Loco Yard	6.30 p.m.	//
6.35 p.m.	Wadebridge	—	
	Station and Quay F Shunting		
	6.35 a.m. to 8.0 a.m.		
	8.20 a.m. to 11.40 a.m.		
	12.10 p.m. to 5.30 p.m.		
	(Less 1 hr. C shunting).		
—	Wadebridge Yard	5.30 p.m.	//
5.35 p.m.	Loco Yard	—	

Wadebridge Men.

(1)   1st set on duty 4.30 a.m., prepare No. 646 duty and then own duty and relief 12.15 p.m.

(2)   Off No. 646, relieve 12.15 p.m., to 1.53 p.m.

(3)   2nd set on duty 1.38 p.m., work, dispose **(S.X.)** relieve No. 587 at 6.55 p.m. work, dispose **(S.O.)** relieve No. 597 at 7.47 p.m. work and dispose.

WADEBRIDGE DUTY No. 647
1 F.T. (13 XX Class)
SATURDAYS EXCEPTED

—	Loco Yard	9.25 a.m.	//
9.30 a.m.	Wadebridge	9.35 a.m.	F
12.41 p.m.	Wenford	—	
F – Shunting 12.45 p.m. to 1.20 p.m.			
—	Wenford	1.20 p.m.	F
3.58 p.m.	Wadebridge	4. 3 p.m.	//
4. 8 p.m.	Loco Yard	—	

Wadebridge Men.

(1)   1st set **(S.X.)** on duty 8.40 a.m., work and commence disposal.

(2)   **S.X.** — Off No. 588, complete disposal

WADEBRIDGE DUTY No. 646
2 P.T./2 F.T. (L.M.R. Class)

—	Loco Yard	6.25 a.m.	//
6.30 a.m.	Wadebridge	6.55 a.m.	P
7.17 a.m.	Bodmin Gen	7.27 a.m.	P
8. 0 a.m.	Padstow	8.12 a.m.	P
8.53 a.m.	Bodmin Gen	8.58 a.m.	P
9.16 a.m.	Wadebridge	9.50 a.m.	P
10.10 a.m.	Bodmin North	11.20 a.m.	P
11.39 a.m.	Wadebridge	11.42 a.m.	P
11.47 a.m.	Loco. Yard	12.18 pm.	//
12.23 p.m.	Wadebridge	12.25 p.m.	P
12.45 p.m.	Bodmin North	2. 0 p.m.	P
2.19 p.m.	Wadebridge	2.22 p.m.	//
2.27 p.m.	Loco Yard	3. 0 p.m.	//
3. 8 p.m.	Wadebridge	3. 9 p.m.	P
	(2.52 p.m. Padstow)		
3.29 p.m.	Bodmin North	4.23 p.m.	P
4.55 p.m.	Padstow	5. 2 p.m.	P
5.32 p.m.	Bodmin North	5.44 p.m.	P
6. 3 p.m.	Wadebridge	6.12 p.m.	P
6.50 p.m.	Bodmin Road	8. 0 p.m.	P
8.52 p.m.	Padstow	9. 0 p.m.	P
9. 9 p.m.	Wadebridge	* *//	
**	Wadebridge Loco	—	

Wadebridge Men.

(1)   Off No. 645, prepare.

(2)   1st set on duty 6.10 a.m., relieved 11.47 a.m., relieve No. 645 at 12.15 p.m. and relieved 1.53 p.m.

(3)   Off No. 591, relieve 11.47 a.m., and relieved 2.30 p.m.

(4)   2nd set on duty 2.15 p.m., work and dispose.

(5)   **S.X.** – Off No. 597, dispose.

Explanatory notes

F	Freight	MO	Mondays only
P	Passenger	MX	Mondays excepted
//	Light engine	SO	Saturdays only
		SX	Saturdays excepted

Extract from local trip working – St. Blazey area June 1971

LAIRA 729 350 h.p. Cl. (08) Mondays to Fridays

ST. BLAZEY TURN NOS. 111, 112

	Arr	Dep	
St. Blazey S. Pt.		04//10	L D M-F
St. Blazey Yard..	04//15	04.25	Frt. 9
Bodmin Road...	05.13	05.25	
Bodmin General...	06.00	06.25	
Boscarne Junction...	06.40	06.56	
Wadebridge	07.24	08.25	
Bodmin General...	09.26	09.34	
Bodmin Road...	09.55	11.11	
Bodmin General...	11.36	11.45	
Boscarne Junction...	12.00		
EITHER			
Boscarne Jcn		12.16	
Wenford...	13.10	14.08	
Boscarne Jcn	15.06	15.22	
Bodmin General...	15.45	15.53	
Bodmin Road...	16.14	16.28	
St. Blazey Yard..	17.09	17//16	LD
St. Blazey S. Pt.	17//21		
OR			
Boscarne Jcn.		12.23	
Wenford...	13.17	14.45	
Boscarne Jcn.	15.44	16.09	
Bodmin General...	16.32	16.40	
Bodmin Road...	17.01	17.15	
St. Blazey Yd.	18.14	18//21	LD
St. Blazey S. Pt.	18//26		

APPENDIX SIX – WORKING INSTRUCTIONS

Southern Railway (Western Section) Appendix to the Working Timetables March 1934

WADEBRIDGE

Cattle dock. – Bogie coaches must not be shunted into the cattle dock siding.

Sand Dock siding and lift bridge. – This siding is connected with one of the sidings at the west end of Wadebridge station and is extended alongside the sand dock.

A lift bridge is provided at the eastern end of the sand dock. This bridge is fitted with a locking bolt operated by a hand lever and, before movements are made over the siding leading to the sand dock, care must be taken to see that the bridge is in its proper position and is secured by the locking bolt.

The bridge has to be lifted manually with the assistance of balance weights suspended on chains, and when it is necessary for barges to pass into or out of the sand dock the bridge must be lifted sufficiently clear to enable such vessels to pass under it.

When high tides are expected care must be taken to leave the bridge unlocked in order to admit of it being automatically lifted by the rising tide, and the Station Foreman when on duty, or other member of the staff deputed by the Station Master, will be held responsible for satisfying himself that this duty has been attended to.

BETWEEN WADEBRIDGE AND BODMIN

Boscarne Junction. – When the line is not clear from Boscarne Junction to Bodmin, the Driver of a S.R. train must draw in clear of the junction points when instructed to do so by the Signalman, and stop there until the line is clear and he has received the tablet to proceed to Bodmin.

BODMIN

The engine performing shunting operations at the Wadebridge end of the station must always be attached at the Wadebridge end of the vehicles it is moving.

Passenger coaches must not be shunted into the cattle dock siding.

WENFORD MINERAL LINE

Traffic is conveyed to and from the line by the mineral train from Wadebridge, and the Guard of this train will be responsible for the proper working of the points.

Only one engine in steam is allowed on the line at one time, and as the branch is not provided with signals, fencing or any protection, a train passing over it must be moved at such a speed that it can be stopped promptly before reaching any obstruction that may be observed on the line by the Enginemen.

Trains must pass over this line only during daylight.

Six-wheeled vehicles must not be permitted to work over this line.

Dunmere crossing. – Before a mineral train passes over the road from Bodmin to Wadebridge at Dunmere crossing, situated at the foot of Dunmere Hill, it must be brought to a stand and the engine whistle sounded freely. The Guard must also stand at the crossing, in good view of the roadway, and exhibit a red flag until the train has passed over the crossing, as a warning to motorists descending the hill.

Tresarrett Quarry Co's siding. – A scotch block is provided on the siding side of the gate.

The men in charge of the mineral train before using the siding must be careful to remove the scotch block from the rail, close the catch points and secure them in that position by padlock whilst shunting is in progress, and when the work has been completed the points must be returned to their normal position and re-locked.

Vehicles for the siding must be placed immediately behind the scotch block in the siding, and those from the siding must be accepted at that point.

The responsibility for the movement of vehicles over the siding beyond the Company's boundary will rest with the Tresarrett Quarry Company, and in no circumstances must the Company's engine pass beyond the exchange point referred to.

Wagons higher that 9 feet above rail must not be permitted to pass under the loading bins at this siding.

English China Clay Company's siding. – This siding has connections to the Wenford line at either end, and two other connections about midway in the siding.

The men in charge of the mineral train when using the siding must be careful to close the catch point at the Wenford end and secure it in that position by padlock whilst shunting is in progress at that end of the siding, and when the work has been completed, all the points leading from the siding must be locked in position to prevent vehicles running foul of the main line.

Wenford Bridge terminus. – There are several sidings at this terminus with points leading into them facing for trains approaching from Boscarne Junction.

A single tongue runaway catch point, facing for trains from Wenford, exists in the single line about ¼ mile from Wenford Bridge terminus, which is normally left open and secured in that position by padlock, the key of which is kept by the Guard of the mineral train.

The Driver of a mineral train must be careful to stop before reaching this catch point, and the Guard must unlock and close the point to admit of the train passing over it safely, afterwards re-locking it in its normal position.

De Lank Quarries (T. W. Ward) siding. - The siding crosses a roadway immediately outside the Company's boundary, the route thence being by a steep incline to the De Lank Quarries, the gradient of which is 1 in 8 rising to the quarries.

The points farthest away from Wenford connecting with No. 1 catch siding are fitted with a spring lever and lie normally for No. 1 catch siding. The points leading to No. 3 catch siding (nearest Wenford) must lie normally for that siding and must be secured in that position by a padlock, the key of which is kept in the goods office at Wenford Bridge terminus.

The Company's engine must not proceed on to the siding beyond the Company's boundary. Outgoing wagons, after being moved by hand into the siding by Messrs. Ward's employees to a point between the Company's boundary and the hand points leading to the siding, must be drawn there from by the Company's engine. Ingoing wagons are berthed in the Company's middle siding, and on application by Messrs. Ward's employees are either moved by engine power or pushed by hand over the points leading to the Quarries' siding and hauled thence by the firm's horses through that siding to the incline.

Not more than two wagons must be worked either up, or down, the De Lank incline at any one time.

Before any wagons are placed upon or taken from the Company's siding leading to the private sidings, the key of the padlock securing the points leading to No. 3 catch siding will be obtained by Messrs. Ward's employees from the Goods Clerk at Wenford, who will be held responsible for satisfying himself that the exchange of wagons can be carried out with safety. He must also satisfy himself that the points leading to No. 3 catch siding are not set for the Company's sidings until trucks which have been lowered from the incline have come to rest at the foot of the incline.

The Goods Clerk will also be responsible for satisfying himself that the points are correctly set for the catch sidings, secured by padlock in that position and the key returned to him as soon as the exchange of wagons has been completed.

LIST OF INTERMEDIATE AND OTHER SIDINGS

Name of siding.	Position.	(1) Station in charge of working. (2) wagons labelled to.†	Gradient at point of connection (1 in)	Catch points provided in sidings at	Points of siding controlled by or worked from	If gates provided across siding — Key to be obtained from	If gates provided across siding — Key to be returned to	Worked by	Remarks
Wadebridge Quay	Up side between Padstow and Wadebridge	Wadebridge	Level	–	Wadebridge West box	Wadebridge West box		Shunting engine	
			WADEBRIDGE EAST TO BODMIN.						
Nanstallon	Up side between Wadebridge and Bodmin	(1) Wadebridge (2) Nanstallon siding	440 falling towards Wadebridge	41 yards from main line	Ground frame. Train Tablet and release lever in Nanstallon Crossing box	Guard of mineral Train		Up and down mineral trains	
Boscarne Jct. No. 1 (Exchange)	Boscarne Jct, between G.W. and S. Bodmin lines.	Wadebridge (siding used for exchange traffic between G.W. and S. Rlys.)	250 Wadebridge end and 196 Bodmin end falling towards Wadebridge	At Bodmin end 47 yards and at Wadebridge end 45 yards from main line	Bodmin end ground frame. Train Tablet. G.W.R. connection ground frame, controlled from box. Wadebridge end worked from Boscarne Jct. box.	–	–	G.W.R. goods services and S.R. mineral train	
Boscarne Jct. No 2	Down side Boscarne Jct.	Wadebridge (for berthing loaded and empty wagons to and from Wenford line)	250 Wadebridge end and 196 Bodmin end falling towards Wadebridge	At Bodmin end 50 yards and at Wadebridge end 61 yards from main line	Bodmin end Dunmere Jct. ground frame. Train Tablet. Wadebridge end worked from Boscarne Jct box	–	–	G.W.R. goods services and S.R. mineral trains	

WENFORD MINERAL LINE.

Location	Position	Name	Gradient	Distance	Points / Frame	Guard	Trains	Remarks
Wenford Mineral Line	Down side Dunmere Jct.	Wadebridge	50 falling towards Wadebridge	60 yards from main line	Ground frame. Train Tablet	Guard of mineral train	Mineral trains	
Dunmere Wharf	Down side between Dunmere Jct. and Wenford	(1) Wadebridge (2) Dunmere Wharf, Wenford	236 falling towards Wadebridge	—	Hand points (padlocked, key held by Guard).	—	Mineral trains	
Helland Wharf	Down side between Dunmere Jct. and Wenford	(1) Wadebridge (2) Helland Wharf, Wenford	673 falling towards Wadebridge	—	Hand points (padlocked, key held by Guard).	—	Mineral trains	
Tresarrett Quarry Co.	Down side between Dunmere Jct. and Wenford	(1) Wadebridge (2) Tresarrett Quarry siding, Wenford	282 falling towards Dunmere Jct.	40 yards from mainline. Scotch block on siding side of gate.	Hand points (padlocked, keys held by Guard).	Guard of mineral train	Mineral trains	
Parkyn	Up side between Wenford and Dunmere Jct.	(1) Wadebridge (2) Parkyn's siding, Wenford	282 falling towards Wadebridge	—	Hand points (padlocked, keys held by Guard).	—	Mineral trains	
Tresarrett Wharf	Down side between Dunmere Jct. and Wenford	(1) Wadebridge (2) Tresarrett Wharf, Wenford	177 falling towards Wadebridge	—	Hand points (padlocked, keys held by Guard).	—	Mineral trains	Connection from running line at both ends of siding
English China Clay Co.	Up side between Wenford and Dunmere Jct.	(1) Wadebridge (2) Clay Co's siding, Wenford	147 falling towards Dunmere Jct.	Wenford end, 65 yards from main line	Hand points (padlocked, keys held by Guard).	—	Mineral trains	Connection from running line at both ends of siding
Wenford Bridge Terminus	Sidings on both sides of single line	(1) Wadebridge (2) Wenford	147 falling towards Dunmere Jct.	—	Hand points (padlocked, keys held by Guard).	—	Mineral trains	
De Lank Quarries (T. W. Ward)	Up side Wenford Bridge	(1) Wadebridge (2) Wenford	Level	3 short catch sidings foot of incline	Hand points in back road siding	Employees of Messrs. Ward, Ltd.	—	

BRITISH RAILWAYS SOUTHERN REGION SECTIONAL APPENDIX TO THE WORKING TIMETABLE OCTOBER 1960

WADEBRIDGE

GOODS SHED. – Locomotives must not enter the goods shed.

VEHICLE RESTRICTION. – Bogie coaches must not be worked into the cattle dock siding.

WADEBRIDGE EAST TO BODMIN NORTH.

WADEBRIDGE.

CONVEYANCE OF TANK WAGONS BY MIXED TRAINS – RULE 240. When a freight train is not available, loaded or empty tank wagons for inflammable and highly inflammable liquids may be conveyed by mixed trains between Wadebridge and Bodmin North marshalled next inside the rear brake van. At least one ordinary freight wagon must be placed between vehicles containing passengers, or readily combustible traffic such as hay or straw, and the tank wagons.

NANSTALLON HALT.

BOSCARNE No. 1 SIDING. – This siding is on the up side (from Bodmin) of the single line at Boscarne Junction with access by a facing connection for down (from Wadebridge) trains. The points are operated from Boscarne Junction signal box. Access is also available at the Bodmin end of the siding by a facing connection for up (from Bodmin) trains and the points are operated from a ground frame released by electric token.

BOSCARNE No. 2 SIDING. – This siding is on the down (from Wadebridge) side of the single line at Boscarne Junction with access by a facing connection for (from Wadebridge) down trains. The points are operated from Boscarne Junction signal box. Access is also available at the Bodmin end of the siding by a facing connection for up (from Bodmin) trains and the points are operated from Dunmere Junction ground frame released by electric token.

WENFORD MINERAL LINE. – This line is on the down (from Wadebridge) side of the single line between Nanstallon Halt and Dunmere Halt with access by a facing connection for trains from the Wadebridge direction. The points are operated from a ground frame released by electric token.

Only one movement may be made on the line at one time. The line is not fenced and drivers must be prepared to stop short of any obstruction. Movements may be made only during daylight and a 20 ton freight brake van at least must be attached at the rear.

Vehicle restrictions. – The following types of vehicle are prohibited from working over this line:-

(a) 4-wheeled freight brake vans exceeding a wheel base of 12 feet 9 inches and overall length of 23 feet.

(b) passenger vehicles (except those formed in the Officer's inspection train).

(c) **All** 6-wheeled vehicles.

(d) Bogie freight vehicles and bogie freight brake vans exceeding the following dimensions:-

Vehicle	Buffers	Headstocks	Length over:- Bogie centres	Bogie wheel base	Total wheel base
Bogie vehicle	48' 0"	45' 0"	35' 6"	5' 6"	41' 0"
Bogie brake van	39' 11"	36' 6"	21' 0"	8' 0"	29' 0"

Dunmere Crossing. – Before a movement passes over the public highway at Dunmere crossing it must be stopped and the engine whistle sounded. The guard must stand at the crossing and exhibit a red flag until the movement has passed over.

English China Clay Lovering Pochin Co., Ltd, Siding. – The guard must be careful to close the trap point at the Wenford end and secure it in that position by padlock whilst shunting is in progress at that end of the siding and, when the work has been completed, see that all the points leading from the siding have been locked in the normal position.

Loading of clay on running line. – A wheel scotch is provided in the running line at a point opposite the Clay Company's kilns to enable empty wagons to be placed thereon for subsequent loading with bagged clay. The working is to be carried out strictly in accordance with the following instructions:-

The booked freight train from Wenford to Wadebridge will, on its departure from and after completion of its work in the firm's sidings, draw out and leave on the running line not more than 6 empty wagons. The gradient of the line is 1 in 147 falling towards Dunmere Junction, and when the train and wagons have come to a stand, the hand brakes on all the wagons must be firmly applied before being detached from the train. The train may then be drawn forward clear of the wheel scotch, which must then be locked across the rail and the key taken by the guard and handed to the station master at Wadebridge.

The guard of the booked freight train from Wadebridge to Wenford must obtain the key of the wheel scotch from the station master at Wadebridge before departure. The train must be brought to a stand clear of the scotch, and when this has been turned clear of the line, the train may propel the wagons to the firm's sidings from where they will be taken to Wadebridge by the return freight service.

Wenford Bridge. – There are several sidings at this terminus with points leading into them facing for trains approaching from Boscarne Junction.

A single tongue catch point, facing for trains from Wenford, exists in the single line ¼ mile from Wenford Bridge and is normally left open and secured in that position by padlock. The driver must be careful to stop before reaching this catch point and the guard must unlock and close the point to admit of the train passing over it safely,afterwards re-locking it in its normal position.

BODMIN NORTH.

SHUNTING. - Vehicles must not be propelled in the Wadebridge direction during shunting operations at the West end of the station.

VEHICLE RESTRICTION. – Passenger coaches must not be worked into the cattle dock siding.

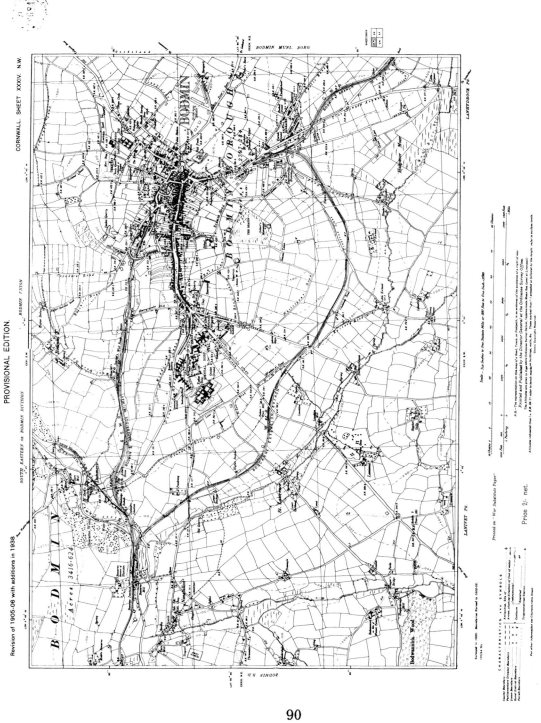

Bodmin and Boscarne from the Ordnance Survey of 1908. The original course of the railway in the Dunmere area can be seen.

90

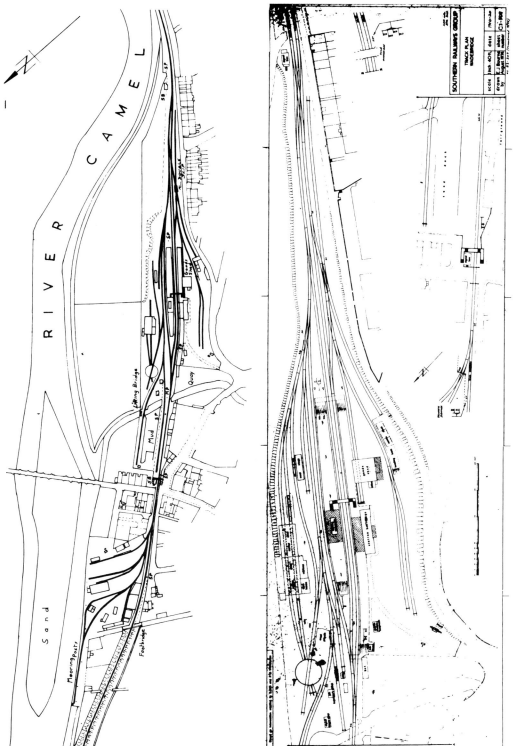

Wadebridge: the layout between 1899 and 1906 (above), and after the abolition of Wadebridge Junction and extension to the locomotive depot.

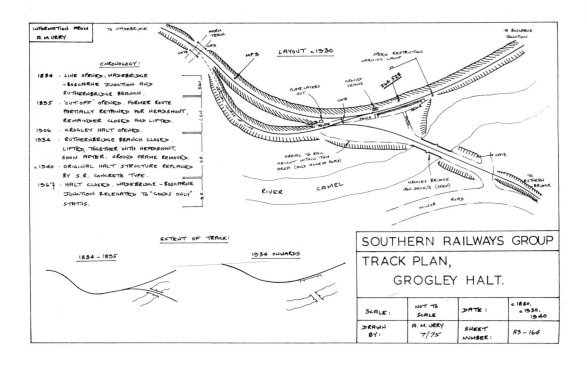

INFORMATION FROM A. M URRY

TO WADEBRIDGE FARM TRACK GATE GATE MP.3 LAYOUT c1930 SPEED RESTRICTION WARNING LAMP TO BOSCARNE JUNCTION

CHRONOLOGY:

1834 - LINE OPENED; WADEBRIDGE -BOSCARNE JUNCTION AND RUTHERNBRIDGE BRANCH.

1895 - 'CUT-OFF' OPENED, FORMER ROUTE PARTIALLY RETAINED FOR HEADSHUNT, REMAINDER CLOSED AND LIFTED.

1906 - GROGLEY HALT OPENED.

1934 - RUTHERNBRIDGE BRANCH CLOSED. LIFTED, TOGETHER WITH HEADSHUNT, SOON AFTER. GROUND FRAME REMOVED.

c1940 - ORIGINAL HALT STRUCTURE REPLACED BY S.R. CONCRETE TYPE.

1967 - HALT CLOSED. WADEBRIDGE - BOSCARNE JUNCTION RELEGATED TO "GOODS ONLY" STATUS.

PLATE LAYERS HUT GROUND FRAME GATE 364 588 FENCE

GRAVEL TO RAIL HEIGHT WITHIN THIS AREA (AND ACCESS ROAD)

RIVER CAMEL

GROGLEY BRIDGE IRON DECK/2 (SKEW)

MINOR ROAD

GATE

TO RUTHERN BRIDGE

EXTENT OF TRACK:

1834 - 1895   1934 ONWARDS

SOUTHERN RAILWAYS GROUP		
TRACK PLAN, GROGLEY HALT.		
SCALE:	NOT TO SCALE	DATE: c1880, c1930, 1940
DRAWN BY:	A. M. URRY 7/75	SHEET NUMBER: A3 - 164

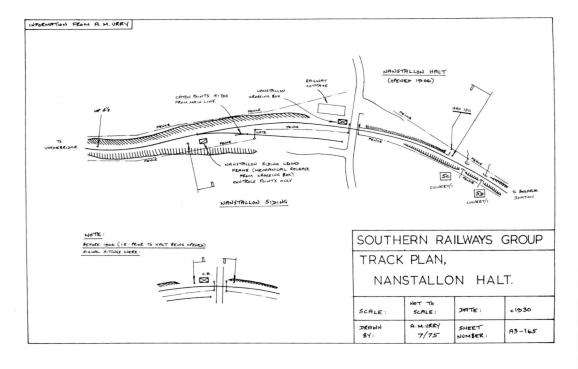

INFORMATION FROM A. M. URRY

CATCH POINTS 41 YDS FROM MAIN LINE NANSTALLON CROSSING BOX RAILWAY COTTAGE NANSTALLON HALT (OPENED 1906)

MP 6½

TO WADEBRIDGE FENCE FENCE GATE FENCE FENCE 440 150 FENCE

NANSTALLON SIDING GROUND FRAME (MECHANICAL RELEASE FROM CROSSING BOX) CONTROLS POINTS ONLY

NANSTALLON SIDING

5C CULVERT/1 5D CULVERT/1 FENCE TO BOSCARNE JUNCTION

NOTE:

BEFORE 1906 (I.E. PRIOR TO HALT BEING OPENED) SIGNAL SITINGS WERE:

C.B.

SOUTHERN RAILWAYS GROUP		
TRACK PLAN, NANSTALLON HALT.		
SCALE:	NOT TO SCALE:	DATE: c1930
DRAWN BY:	A. M. URRY 7/75	SHEET NUMBER: A3-165

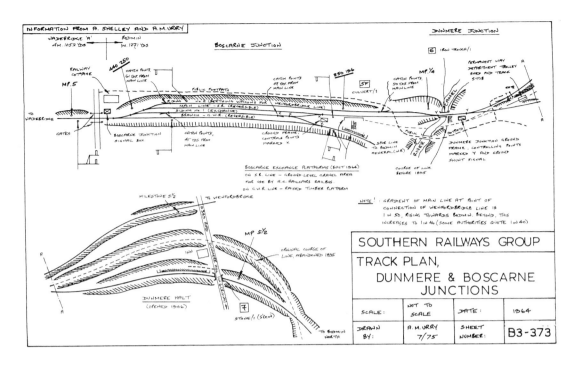

SOUTHERN RAILWAYS GROUP

TRACK PLAN,
DUNMERE & BOSCARNE
JUNCTIONS

SCALE:	NOT TO SCALE	DATE:	1964
DRAWN BY:	A.M.URRY 7/75	SHEET NUMBER:	B3-373

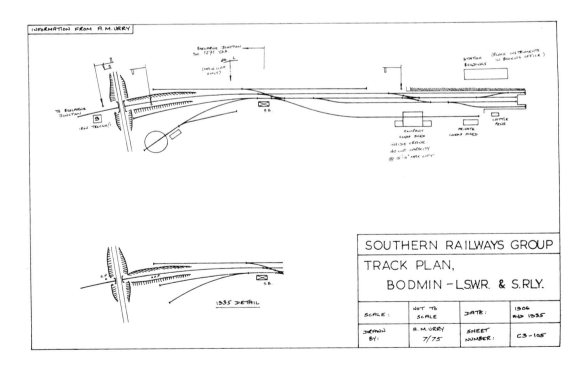

SOUTHERN RAILWAYS GROUP

TRACK PLAN,
BODMIN – L.S.W.R. & S.RLY.

SCALE:	NOT TO SCALE	DATE:	1906 AND 1935
DRAWN BY:	A.M.URRY 7/75	SHEET NUMBER:	C3-105

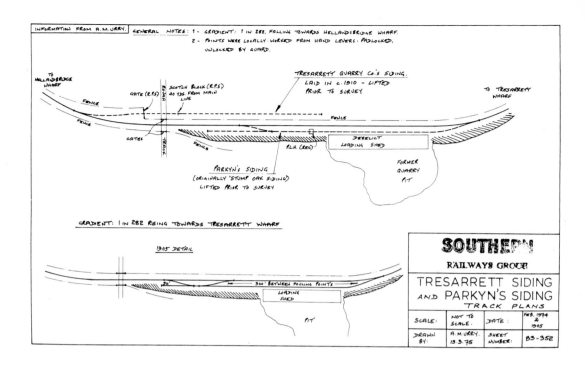

GENERAL NOTES: 1 - GRADIENT: 1 IN 282, FALLING TOWARDS HELLANDSBRIDGE WHARF.
2 - POINTS WERE LOCALLY WORKED FROM HAND LEVERS: PADLOCKED,
UNLOCKED BY GUARD.

TO HELLANDSBRIDGE WHARF

FENCE

GATE (R.P.S.)

SCOTCH BLOCK (R.P.S.)
40 YDS. FROM MAIN LINE

TRESARRETT QUARRY CO's SIDING.
LAID IN c.1910 - LIFTED
PRIOR TO SURVEY

TO TRESARRETT WHARF

FENCE

FENCE

GATES

TRACK

FENCE

P.L.H. (REC)

DERELICT
LOADING SHED

FORMER QUARRY PIT

PARKYN'S SIDING
(ORIGINALLY 'STUMP OAK SIDING)
LIFTED PRIOR TO SURVEY

GRADIENT: 1 IN 282 RISING TOWARDS TRESARRETT WHARF

1905 DETAIL

30'

300' BETWEEN FOULING POINTS

LOADING SHED

PIT

SOUTHERN
RAILWAYS GROUP

TRESARRETT SIDING
AND PARKYN'S SIDING
TRACK PLANS

SCALE:	NOT TO SCALE.	DATE:	FEB. 1974 & 1905
DRAWN BY:	A.M.URRY. 13.3.75	SHEET NUMBER:	B3-352

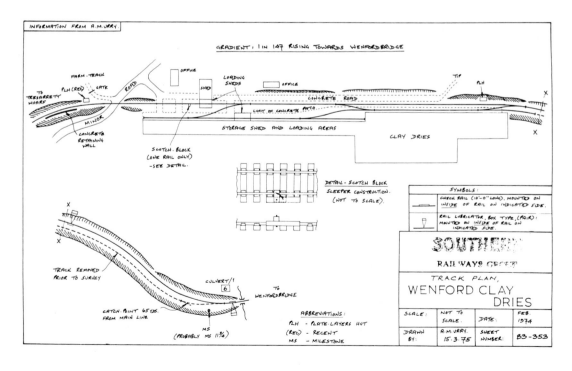

GRADIENT: 1 IN 147 RISING TOWARDS WENFORDBRIDGE

FARM TRACK

OFFICE

LOADING SHEDS

OFFICE

TIP

P.L.H.

TO TRESARRETT WHARF

P.L.H. (REC)

GATE

ROAD

SHED

CONCRETE ROAD

X

MINOR

CONCRETE RETAINING WALL

LIMIT OF CONCRETE PATIO

STORAGE SHED AND LOADING AREAS

CLAY DRIES

X

SCOTCH BLOCK
(ONE RAIL ONLY)
- SEE DETAIL.

DETAIL - SCOTCH BLOCK
SLEEPER CONSTRUCTION.
(NOT TO SCALE).

SYMBOLS:

CHECK RAIL (10'-0" LONG), MOUNTED ON INSIDE OF RAIL ON INDICATED SIDE.

RAIL LUBRICATOR, BOX TYPE, (PAIR): MOUNTED ON INSIDE OF RAIL ON INDICATED SIDE.

X

X

TRACK REMOVED
PRIOR TO SURVEY

CULVERT/1
6

TO WENFORDBRIDGE

CATCH POINT 65 YDS.
FROM MAIN LINE.

MS
(PROBABLY MS 11¾)

ABBREVIATIONS:

PLH - PLATE LAYERS HUT

(REC) - RECENT

MS - MILESTONE

SOUTHERN
RAILWAYS GROUP

TRACK PLAN,
WENFORD CLAY
DRIES

SCALE:	NOT TO SCALE.	DATE:	FEB. 1974
DRAWN BY:	A.M.URRY. 15.3.75	SHEET NUMBER:	B3-353

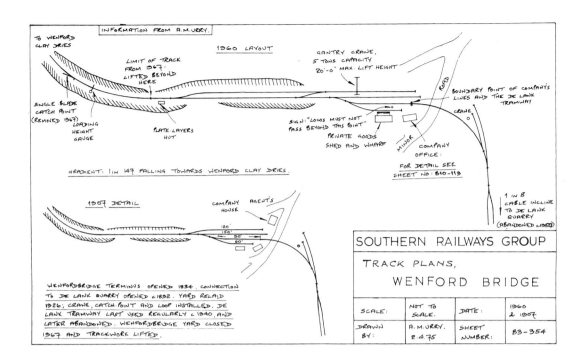

INFORMATION FROM A.M. URRY.

1960 LAYOUT

TO WENFORD
CLAY DRIES

LIMIT OF TRACK
FROM 1967:
LIFTED BEYOND
HERE

GANTRY CRANE,
5 TONS CAPACITY
20'-0" MAX. LIFT HEIGHT

BOUNDARY POINT OF COMPANY'S
LINES AND THE DE LANK
TRAMWAY

SINGLE BLADE
CATCH POINT
(REMOVED 1967)

LOADING
HEIGHT
GAUGE

PLATE-LAYERS
HUT

SIGN: "LOCOS MUST NOT
PASS BEYOND THIS POINT"

PRIVATE GOODS
SHED AND WHARF

CRANE

MINOR
ROAD

COMPANY
OFFICE:
FOR DETAIL SEE
SHEET NO: B10-119

1 IN 8
CABLE INCLINE
TO DE LANK
QUARRY
(ABANDONED CLOSED)

GRADIENT: 1 IN 147 FALLING TOWARDS WENFORD CLAY DRIES.

1907 DETAIL

COMPANY
HOUSE

AGENT'S

120'
150'
30'
60'

WENFORDBRIDGE TERMINUS OPENED 1834. CONNECTION
TO DE LANK QUARRY OPENED c1832. YARD RELAID
1826; CRANE, CATCH-POINT AND LOOP INSTALLED. DE
LANK TRAMWAY LAST USED REGULARLY c 1840, AND
LATER ABANDONED. WENFORDBRIDGE YARD CLOSED
1967 AND TRACKWORK LIFTED.

SOUTHERN RAILWAYS GROUP			
TRACK PLANS, WENFORD BRIDGE			
SCALE:	NOT TO SCALE.	DATE:	1960 & 1907
DRAWN BY:	A.M. URRY. 2.4.75	SHEET NUMBER:	B3-354

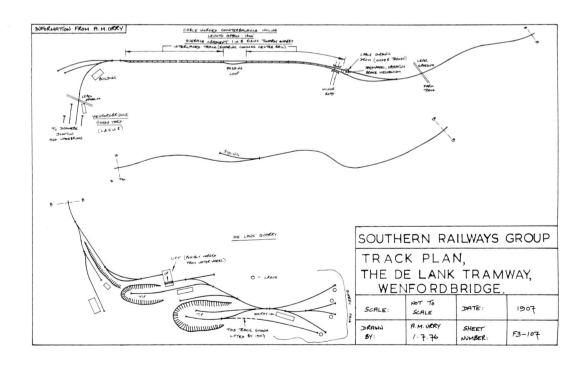

INFORMATION FROM A.M. URRY.

CABLE WORKED COUNTERBALANCE INCLINE
LENGTH APPROX. 1300'
AVERAGE GRADIENT 1 IN 8 RISING TOWARDS QUARRY
INTERLACED TRACK (SHARING COMMON CENTRE RAIL)

CABLE WINDING
FROM (UNDER TRACKS)

HANDWHEEL OPERATING
BRAKE MECHANISM

LEVEL
CROSSING

BUILDING

LEVEL
CROSSING

PASSING
LOOP

MINOR
ROAD

FARM
TRACK

WENFORDBRIDGE
GOODS YARD
(L.S.W.R.)

TO DUNMERE
JUNCTION
AND WADEBRIDGE

SIDING

B — B

B

B

B — B

DE LANK QUARRY

LIFT (ASHLEY WORKED
FROM WATER WHEEL)

O = CRANE

TIP

TIP

TIP

SMITHY

THIS TRACK SHOWN
LIFTED BY 1907

QUARRY FACE

QUARRY FACE

SOUTHERN RAILWAYS GROUP			
TRACK PLAN, THE DE LANK TRAMWAY, WENFORDBRIDGE.			
SCALE:	NOT TO SCALE	DATE:	1907
DRAWN BY:	A.M. URRY 1.7.76	SHEET NUMBER:	F3-107

AUTHOR'S NOTE

It is over twenty years since the Third Edition of this book was published and in that time the trains have disappeared from the Bodmin & Wadebridge Railway and the track lifted, though at the time of writing (January 1994) a public enquiry into reopening the Wenford line was pending. The author is indebted to the many people who have helped in the compilation of this book, especially the late D. L. Bradley for permission to use material from his book "Locomotives of the LSWR" (published by the Railway Correspondence & Travel Society) and for supplying information of the early locomotive history of the B&WR; the late W. E. Hayward; The Editor, West Briton & Cornwall Advertiser; the then Archivist, British Railways Board, whose collection of the company's minute books and much else of interest is now in the Public Records Office, Kew; British Railways Southern and Western Regions; Cornwall County Archivist; J&M Dent Ltd, for permission to publish extracts from Sir Arthur Quiller-Couch's "Cuckoo Valley Railway"; J.R.W. Kirkby; M. Dart and A. Croft of the Bodmin & Wenford Railway.

ILLUSTRATIONS

The following have kindly supplied photographs: Bodmin Museum (p.54 below); Brunel University Locomotive Collection* (p.43 below); the late H. C. Casserley (p.31 top, 35 below, 53 top); R. M. Casserley (p.32 below); M. J. Esau (p.33 top, 36 below); M. Farr (p.34 top); Locomotive & General Railway Photographs (p.11, 12, 21 top, 25 top, 26 top & below, 38 top, 42 top, 49, 50 top); S. C. Nash (34 below, 35 top); R. C. Riley (p.32 below); F. H. Casbourn, courtesy of the Stephenson Locomotive Society (p.43 top, 46); P. Q. Treloar (p.21 below, 22 below, 30 below); J. Vaughan collection (p.36 top, 38 below). Those on p.22 (top), 25 (centre & below), 26 (centre), 27, 30 (top), 31 (below), 32 (top), 33 (below), 37 (top) and 50 (below) are by the author. The map on p.6 was specially drawn by F. J. Mackett. The plans on pages 91-95 are reproduced by permission of the Southern Railways Group.

* Brunel University Collection photographs are available from 3 Fairway, Clifton, York YO3 6AQ.

Printed and bound by Short Run Press, Exeter.